19

D1569567

B
RIC   Rich, Mary.
              Evil web.

$22.95

DATE			

evil
web

A TRUE STORY OF CULT
ABUSE AND COURAGE

evil
web

MARY RICH

AND

CAROL JOSE

New Horizon Press   Far Hills, NJ

Requests for permission should be addressed to:
New Horizon Press
P.O. Box 669
Far Hills, NJ 07931

Rich, Mary and Jose, Carol
        Evil Web: A True Story of Cult Abuse and Courage

Library of Congress Catalog Card Number: Pending

ISBN: 0-88282-139-3

New Horizon Press

Manufactured in the U.S.A.

2000 1999 1998 1997 1996 / 5 4 3 2 1

To the innocent children . . . everywhere.

"Terrors arc turned upon me:
They pursue my soul as the wind:
And my welfare passeth away as a cloud."

Job 30:15

contents

acknowledgments

Books today are rarely the result of an author sitting alone in a garret, yellow pad and number two pencil in hand. Nor was this one.

Our gratitude goes to the following: Larry Guarino, whose book *A POW'S Story: 2801 Days in Hanoi* (Ivy/Random House, 1990) was the catalyst that brought us together to write this story; special friend, guiding light, and literary agent Ray Nugent of Naples, Florida; Dr. Robert Cross, psychotherapist, of Indian Harbour Beach, Florida for professional guidance and the Afterword; critical first reader and faithful assistant, Linda Downie; Randall Larrinaga for his insights and experiences; our computer guru Michael Herman; and Todd Robert Poch, PsyD. MALD, of Denver Colorado.

We'd like to thank Bob McDonald, Theresa DeCapua, Craig Bailey, and Melinda Meers of *FLORIDA TODAY*. We also thank Joan Dunphy and Dennis McCarthy of New Horizon Press for their encouragement and able assistance.

Most of all, we are grateful to Dale Jose, Lou Francavilla, and our families, who were always there with patience and love, and generous with moral, and emotional and financial support when we needed it during the more than four years spent in seeing this book through from first word to publication.

author's note

This book is based on the experiences of Mary Rich and reflects her perceptions of the past, present, and future. The personalities, events, actions, and conversations portrayed within the story have been taken from her memory, extensive interviews, research, court documents, letters, personal papers, press accounts, and the memories of participants.

To safeguard the privacy of certain individuals, the author has changed their names and the names of certain places and, in some cases, altered identifying relations or characteristics. Events involving the characters happened as described; only minor details have been changed.

prologue

I stood at rigid attention at the back of the bedroom closet, facing the wall, hands behind my back, barely daring to breathe. Sweat beaded up on my body, and the tiny drops prickled as they detached themselves and went sliding down my scalp, down the sides of my nose, down between my breasts, down the inside of my legs. I had been standing there like that for hours.

The urge to move, to wipe away the drops of sweat, to turn and run was agonizing. I prayed. "Please, God, help me. Help me be obedient. Save me from more punishment."

Here and there, a faint sound told me that the household was stirring. I stole a glance sideways. The neat rows of empty clothes on their hangers seemed like watchful sentinels, waiting for me to make a wrong move so they could pounce. I held my breath, not daring to move. I felt dizzy, and feared I would fall.

I seemed to be operating in thick mists of fog that shrouded my focus and my perspective, even my ability to function. It was about eight o'clock on a Saturday morning in April, but I didn't know that. I had long ago lost track of days and hours.

Consigned to the dimness of the closet in that small suburban house in Palm Cay, Florida, I felt only cold and numbness on my bare feet and legs, heat in the rest of my body, and pain. Always pain. And hunger and thirst. Food and water were frequently withheld as punishment, and we were fed only sparingly otherwise. There were many mouths to feed, and we were always too poor, or so we were told.

Dishes clattered in the kitchen. I breathed in lightly, and the smell of coffee slid up my nostrils, bringing saliva into my mouth. Coffee! Hunger wrenched my stomach. Stealthily, I shifted one foot slightly, then the other. Sweat ran into my eyes, burning them, and the things around me blurred. Cautiously, I reached up and wiped the sweat away from my face, then brought my hand down to clasp the other hand behind my back as I had been ordered. Surely no one could have seen that one little move, that one little infraction of the rules, I told myself.

Closing my eyes, I prayed again, fervently. "Dear Lord, make me see the error of my ways. Help me to do better. Help me to be worthy enough to be back in Ron's good graces again. Help me to endure this punishment."

If I didn't falter, I might get something to eat this morning. I might not get another beating. I might even get to leave the closet. If I could just hold on long enough, just endure, Kathleen might call me to the kitchen for a bowl of cold oatmeal—a sugarless, choking paste—but welcome, oh so welcome, because with it would come a precious few minutes of freedom, a chance to sit, a brief respite from the hunger pangs gnawing at my belly.

The walls of the bedroom closet had been the boundaries of my world for weeks, maybe even a month now. When I was permitted to sleep, which wasn't often, I dropped to the floor and slept there. Ron liked it when I was banished to the closet for punishment. He would come creeping in, shut the door carefully, order me in a hoarse whisper to lie down, to take off my clothes. Then he'd amuse himself with me, away from the eyes of his wife and the other adults, away from the children's curiosity. I was his creature, totally at his mercy. He could do whatever he wanted to me.

That day, I was wearing the same light cotton dress I'd been wearing for days. Maybe I'll be forgiven today, I dared to hope. Maybe today I'll be allowed to bathe, put on clean clothes.

Some times I fled to the closet on my own, seeking a haven. Mostly, the closet was my cell and no haven at all from the constant, unrelenting beatings or humiliation, as the pain lancing through my feet and the soreness across my back attested.

Suddenly, the door was thrown open. Ron's lieutenant Kathleen came into the closet. "These are Ron's orders," she said. She began to beat me severely on my feet and legs, using a flat piece of dried palm frond from the yard, one that was edged with sharp stickers. It made a whispering sound as she wielded it again and again, with sharp staccato slaps on my bare feet and legs.

I cried out in pain, imploring her to "Stop, oh stop! Please! Don't, ooh! I've repented and will be good." I avowed over and over again, "I'll obey, to please God and do His will." Finally, after what seemed like an eternity, she stopped. I fell in a heap on the closet floor, facing the wall, my body drawn up in a ball, trying to protect my legs, sobbing and whimpering. She added a few sharp swats across my back for good measure.

"Now get up!" she ordered roughly. "Get up and stand facing the wall!" I felt I couldn't move, but I knew that if I didn't the beating would only begin all over again. There were my blood spots on the carpet—some old, some from this morning—that grimly attested to Kathleen's diligence in carrying out Ron's commands. I pulled myself to my knees, then slowly stood on my bruised and swollen feet. Gasping, weeping, I again faced the wall, hands behind my back.

"Stand there now, and repent your sinful behavior!" She left, closing the closet door. I'd be there, I knew, until Ron decided to release me. Or punish me again.

The pain was receding somewhat, but I was close to dropping from exhaustion. Then, "Bang! Bam!" Violent banging came from somewhere near the front of the house. A searing pain ran up my leg, and I cried out, unable to suppress it. Suddenly, there was the sound of running feet in the house. The closet door opened and, some of the children quickly crawled in behind me. They were scurrying for cover. Someone was at the front door. Ron always made the children hide whenever anyone came near the house. The sound of their ragged breathing filled the closet, but none of them spoke. We stood still, all perfectly silent, as we had been taught to be. I could hear more banging at the door, louder now, and then some muffled shouts outside. It sounded like someone was shouting for Ron to open the door. I strained to hear, not daring to move, not daring to turn around. "Go out the back, go around and see who it is!"

Ron's hoarse command to someone came from the safety of the hallway just outside the bedroom. I heard the back door open and slam closed. Open again, slam again. There were whispered consultations in the hall. Then another angrily hissed command from Ron, "Bring Mary here, get Mary out here!"

"Oh, God," I prayed silently. "Oh God, please, please, not me, not now." But Kathleen was already inside the closet. She grabbed my arm and yanked me around to face her.

"Get out there!" she hissed, fixing me with a glare. My heart began to pound with terror. "Ron wants you. In the living room, fast." She shoved me toward the door. I stumbled, limping, to the living room. Ron paced the room, ducking around the windows to avoid being seen from outside. He turned to me with a withering look of accusation, his dark eyes blazing in anger. My heart and stomach contracted with fear.

"It's your husband Jack and my son Randall out there. They want you."

Before I could grasp what he was saying, someone banged mightily on the front door again, shouting, "Open this door! Get this door open! We want to talk to you!" I couldn't really comprehend what was happening. I tried to focus. The pain in my feet was excruciating, I felt cold all over, and I wanted to turn and flee, to seek the warmth of the closet, to hide there with the kids. I knew from the look on Ron's face that whatever was happening, he considered it my fault, and more punishment would surely follow. Waves of fear rippled through my body and cramped my stomach. I thought I was going to faint. I didn't even notice that I had started to wet myself in terror.

Suddenly another command came. "Get out there," demanded Ron in a furious voice. "Tell them to get out of here! Away from this house!" He was crouched down, a gun in his hands, below the windows, well away from the front door. I started toward it, and he hissed, "No! Keep that door locked! Go out the back!"

Oblivious to the throbbing in my feet, spurred on by a greater fear, I stumbled out the back door, past some of the other adults and children, and ran around to the front of the house. After so long in the dark closet, I reeled from the initial impact of the bright daylight. The Florida sun had already detached itself from the horizon and glided up into the sky, coaxing a brilliant green from the ocean's depths and enfolding the day in its heavy, warm embrace. When my eyes adjusted, I saw a bunch of people in the front yard. A van had pulled right up onto the lawn, blocking the driveway. My husband Jack, whom I hadn't seen since we left California over two months before, was there, along with Ron's oldest son Randall. Jack was pounding on the front door like a crazy man. I ran up to him past an official looking man with a salt and pepper crewcut who was standing by the van holding a walkie-talkie.

"Jack!" I screamed, "What do you think you're doing? Go away! We don't want you here!" At the sound of my voice he turned, and, seeing me, grabbed my arm.

"Mary! Thank God! I've come to get you and the kids! I'm taking you out of here. Come on! Get in the van." He was pulling me toward the van parked on the lawn. Frantically, I pulled away.

"No!" I cried. "Leave me alone! Let go of me. We're not going anywhere with you! Get out of here!" I had to get them to go away, to leave us alone, or Ron would surely beat me to death for this. "Go away!" I was sobbing, pleading with him. "Please! You must go! I don't want to go with you!"

"No!" he cried, still pulling me toward the van. "You're my wife and these are my children, and I'm going to take you back with me. You have no right to be here. That man is a madman; he has you under his spell, and I'm taking all of you out of here until you come to your senses!"

Rocking back and forth, I launched quickly into my spiel as Ron had taught me: "You have no right to my life!" I screamed. "I left of my own volition! You're the evil one, Jack! You have shown that you hate God. I left because of the fear of staying with you, because you're a devil worshiper! Get out of here, leave us alone, I *will not* go back with you! Never!"

Jack tried to reason with me. "Mary, Mary," he said more softly, "you've got to listen to me. Please. You've got to get out of here, and get the children out of his grip. Come with me, please, please."

At that, I became hysterical. Slapping wildly at him, I twisted my arm and my body, trying to escape, screaming for them all to leave. Tears ran down my face, and my heart pounded drumlike in my chest and ears. "You have to go, you have to go," I chanted. If I didn't make them leave, Ron would beat me again. I'd never get out of that closet. He'd hate me forever. God would punish me. Ron would punish me.

On that fateful April Saturday, Jack and Randall had tried desperately to pull me out of the emotional and psychological quagmire into which I had sunk, taking my own children with me. But the suppression of all reason, the imprisonment of mind and body which Ron Larrinaga had begun quietly and insidiously years before in California, was total. Though I desperately needed help it could not come from others but only from within myself. It would be many more long and painful months before I'd be able to take the first steps to free myself from the profound and evil personal influence and the continuous physical, sexual, and psychological abuse of Ron Larrinaga, and come to my senses again. It would take another two years before I'd really begin to come to terms with the ugly and irrevocable truth of what had happened to us. It will take a lifetime of searching my soul and questioning to understand how it had all begun.

1

the snake appears

I think I had been searching for religious affirmation since earliest childhood. Ours was an average, middle class California family. We attended the Methodist church on Sundays and I went to Sunday School, but religion was never a daily priority in our household. It existed on Sundays and at Christmas, and my parents were pretty much indifferent about it the rest of the time.

But I felt drawn to God and wanted to learn more about religion. Religious ceremonies and beliefs seemed very mysterious and compelling to me. Our neighborhood was filled with Mexican Catholics whose nearby church intrigued me. I was about nine when I began spying on it from a perch in the pepper tree in the vacant lot across the street. Peering through the deep green leaves into the open door of the church, I could just make out the glitter of gold, bits of intricate carving, and the flickering of candles. It seemed thrilling and exciting. I burned to see it up close. One day, I gathered up my courage and stole inside. Tiptoeing to

the front past several kneeling, black-shawled women praying with beads in their hands, I slid quietly into the front pew
and sat down, expecting any minute to be exposed as an
imposter and thrown out. My heart pounded, but no one
noticed me. Carefully, I looked around. Ivory candles blazed
in front of enormous statues. The one with the most candles
in front of it was a beautiful blue-gowned woman I knew was
supposed to be the mother of Christ. Mary. I was named for
her. Next, I stared closely at the huge crucifix above the altar
and became mesmerized. I winced looking at the nails piercing His hands and feet, the blood dripping from under the
crown of spiky thorns on His head, and more blood running
down from the wound in His chest. I was both drawn to and
repelled by that frightful image. I began to cry at the thought
of such suffering. Bowing my head, I prayed fervently,
telling Christ and His mother how much I loved them and
how much I regretted my sins that caused all their suffering.
"I'll serve you always, in everything I do," I whispered.

I left there that day determined to devote my life to
loving Christ and serving Him in every way I could. I was
disappointed that my family's feeling about religion did not
match the depth of devotion that I longed for. They seemed
indifferent, and they resisted all my attempts to change them.

A few years later, when I was twelve, I met Grace
Alexis and her family. They were born-again Christians.
Grace and I, classmates at school, soon became close friends,
and I spent a lot of time at her house. Her family impressed
upon me their strong spiritual beliefs. I admired the way
Grace's father, a stern and uncompromising man who was
unquestionably the head of his household, read from the
Bible every night at dinner. "Never," he'd say in a deep

sonorous voice which made us shudder in awe as he peered fiercely at us over his reading glasses, "compromise the word of God." Largely through their influence, I became born again, too, and at thirteen I formally pledged my life to Jesus Christ. I was devastated when, a short time later, Grace's father was transferred and her family moved away.

During the next few years I longed constantly for the religious fervor I had enjoyed so briefly in Grace's home during those few years they had lived near our community. Following Grace's father's precepts and unmoved by my parents' concern and the teasing of my older brothers and sister, I totally shunned music, dancing, and dating during my high school years. Instead, I attended Pentecostal meetings and Bible study sessions, and prayed constantly. My future family, I was determined, would be a Christ-centered family, avoiding worldly frivolity and eschewing any compromise of God's word.

By eighteen, I had grown into a tall willowy redhead, a college student with an almost obsessional need for religious affirmation my family still considered far too serious for my years. Despite their pleas for me to enjoy my youth and be more moderate, I continued to seek spiritual perfection.

At twenty I married Jack, a tall, dark-haired serious young man and fellow student, who was studying nights to be a teacher. I dropped out of school when I became pregnant with our first child. By the age of twenty-two I had two children, Philip, nearly two, and our baby, Louise.

It was at about that time, on a rainy Sunday in May, that Ron Larrinaga came into our lives. I first noticed him during services at our church in San Luis Obispo. He and his wife and children were seated in the pew directly across from us, and I saw that he immediately opened his Bible, searched the Scriptures, and read with deep concentration all during the service. He'd look up briefly at the pastor, then back down at his Bible, and I was fascinated at how he was able to give God's word his full and rapt attention, even while the pastor was speaking. His wife next to him seemed as engrossed in the open Bible as he was. Three little children sat quietly on either side of them, and there was a serious-faced baby on the woman's lap. They were such a serene and devout family group that I could scarcely tear my gaze away long enough to pay attention to my own restless family and the service. Our two little ones were whispering and squirming, and Jack and I had to constantly shush them. Whenever I looked over at the other pew, the Larrinaga children never moved or made a sound. I could scarcely believe it.

When the service ended, we all headed over to the Social Hall next door, and, before I knew it, Ron Larrinaga was holding sway over our little group of young married couples. A well-built man of medium height, he had straight dark hair neatly parted and combed back. Piercing dark blue eyes that reminded me of the ocean's unfathomable depths looked out at me from behind wire-rimmed glasses. He quickly introduced himself as we entered the group. Then immediately he went back to witnessing to us and the others, which was not unusual in our religion. He told us about his conversion to Christ and of his decision to commit his life and his family's life to following the will of God in all things. As he spoke in a deep hypnotic voice of his devotion and his faith, his tone softened, his face took on a look of intensity, and tears appeared in his eyes. He seemed visibly shaken by the realization of his transformation. "I just came out of the military," he said, "and we decided to move to California, because one of my former commanding officers, a man of God whom I admired, was from here." He reached out, took my hand and shook it warmly, introducing his wife Janet, who was holding their baby in her arms. The three other Larrinaga children stood shyly next to her, one hanging onto her skirt. The oldest couldn't have been more than five. "This is June," said Ron, pointing to the oldest child, "and this is Bobby, and that's Randall, and this is our baby, Amy."

Touching little Amy, he smiled with great warmth and charm, and I felt myself drawn to him, much as I had been drawn to the sight of his pious family in church.

As I looked around at the group of young men and women, I saw each one staring at this man with rapt attention. To our surprise, he now launched into the story of his childhood. "I was beaten and ignored by my parents," he said quietly, "cast out on the streets to fend for myself, to starve or freeze, from the age of five." I gasped in shock. "My mother died of a tumor on the brain a few years later, and I was sent to an orphanage in New Jersey, which is where I grew up." He told us how he had been harassed and tormented, physically and sexually, by the older and bigger boys at the orphanage. "Once they tied me to a tree, beat me, and left me there, not knowing if I'd live or die." He paused, and I felt him looking at me, and I looked back at him sympathetically. "Fortunately, someone from the orphanage found me there and saved me."

Jack and I caught each other's eye. We couldn't believe the horrifying tale we were hearing. According to Ron, somehow, living sometimes on the streets, sometimes with his father or grandmother, and sometimes in the orphanage, he got through his childhood and teenage years. As the full impact of the cruelty inflicted on him hit us, we gasped in shock and murmured in sympathy. My heart went out to him. What a life he'd had as a child! "God eventually led me to join the Air Force, where I at last found Jesus Christ and accepted Him as my Savior," he concluded. I was astounded by what suffering the man had endured and overcome.

"What a joy and comfort it must be to you and your family to have found Christ after all that and to be able to enfold yourselves in His love," I said softly.

Katie Sue, another of the wives, chimed in, "We welcome you to our community and to our church."

Ron smiled warmly at both of us. I glanced nervously at his children, worried at what they might feel about what we'd just heard from their father, but they remained quiet, listening closely to him, showing no outward signs of restlessness or upset. It didn't occur to me then that their behavior was unnatural for children that young. I was just impressed with how well-behaved they were. What good parents Ron and Janet Larrinaga must be, I thought. Jack and I could certainly learn something from them. They have four children and all are perfectly behaved. We have two who are constantly cutting up. Sometimes they nearly drove me crazy.

As he continued talking, his voice held all of us in sway. He reminded me a lot of Grace's father. Like Grace's father, Ron revealed his deep, sincere devotion to God to us without hesitation or embarrassment, and, in doing so, he showed an astounding command of Scripture. When he spoke of God or quoted Scripture, his voice rose with

14

thundering authority and resounded with sincerity. I found myself trembling, and goose bumps ran along my arms. Ron Larrinaga was a born preacher and leader. He spoke with a fluency and a naturalness that was absolutely spellbinding, and he seemed always able to produce the exact Scriptural quotation to illustrate his point. I stole another glance at Jack. He, too, seemed fascinated by Larrinaga, hanging on his every word, as were the others in our small group.

I became oblivious to all except the man speaking to us with such fervor. I was deaf to everything except his message of a life devoted to Christ. That Sunday, Ron Larrinaga plumbed skillfully the depths of my soul and sounded all of its hidden longing. I was not only fascinated by the man himself, I was seduced by his total devotion to the principles upon which I had long wanted us to base our lives. More than anything, I felt I had at last found the person who could show us the way to the path of righteousness.

Ron paused for a moment in his long speech. I looked at Janet, his wife, and felt a quick pang of sympathy for her. She was a thin, frumpy, rather unattractive woman. There were deep circles under her pale green eyes, which gave her a look of tired resignation. And no wonder! I thought. So many babies, one after the other! She must be worn out. My own two, at barely thirteen months apart, were quite a strain. Janet's dull brown hair hung limp and straight, and her dress, though clean, had seen plenty of wear. On closer inspection, the children looked bedraggled, too. In fact, they all looked as if they hadn't had a good meal in a while. I resolved to invite them for a meal soon. It was the least we could do for them, to show Christian charity. Besides, I wanted to get to know Ron better and hear more of his Christian thinking.

I stole a glance at my watch. Ron had been talking nonstop for more than forty-five minutes! During all that time, his children had stood quietly by, giving their father their full attention. My son Philip was off running around, squealing, laughing, chasing the other youngsters in the room. Louise, our baby, dozed in her stroller next to me, but I knew she'd soon be awake and squalling. I wondered how Ron Larrinaga kept his children under such perfect control. Sometime I wanted to find out what the trick was and emulate him, but at that moment I wanted him to wind up his story so we could leave. Finally, people began interrupting him to say their goodbyes. He looked startled, and slightly annoyed, when they did. I seized that opportunity for us to say our goodbyes, too. "We have to go, but I'm going to invite you to our house real soon," I said. "We'd like to learn more about how you came to your decision to devote your life to Christ."

"Thank you. We'd like that very much." He smiled, took my hand, and looked directly into my eyes. I felt my heart beat a little faster but I said nothing more. Jack corralled Philip, and we left.

Driving home, Jack and I talked about how different the Larrinagas were from anyone we had ever met. I liked them a lot and did not hesitate to voice my admiration for them to my husband. "It's not often," I said, "that you find anyone whose religious convictions carry over into every aspect of their lives. He seems to do that. We could learn a lot from him." Never did I feel so challenged to commit my whole heart to God as I had when Ron Larrinaga described his own devotion to our Lord. Although Jack had listened intently to Larrinaga's words he turned out to be more skeptical about Ron, but I thought it was because Jack was only recently converted and had not grown in Christ for many years, as I had. Nevertheless, I felt annoyed that he did not feel as drawn to Ron as I did.

"You're too cynical," I accused him. "You need to open your heart more to Christ. Ron is obviously a man of great devotion, and a good family man. Look how well-behaved his children are! I think we should invite them over for lunch or dinner, and soon. I don't think they have a lot of money, and as Christians we should invite them to share our table."

"Well, go ahead and invite them. I have no objection if you want to share a meal with them. Let's go ahead and ask them and see if they're really all that committed, or if it's only a Sunday act."

"Oh, don't be such a cynic," I shot back. "You think everyone is as shallow about religion as you are."

After that, though, other things cropped up, and I didn't get around to inviting the Larrinagas. We were terribly busy. Jack was still going to school days and working at the post office at night. The children kept me hopping every day. They got bad colds and so did I, so we didn't get to church the following Sunday, or the one after that. The Larrinagas slipped to the back of our minds. It was almost a month before we ran into them again.

Our church's young married group had planned a progressive dinner party. It would be exciting to go to a different home for each course, and I was really looking forward to it. We were very poor and couldn't afford baby-sitters, so we rarely got to go anywhere. Some of the older members of our church volunteered to baby-sit that evening so we young people could have an evening out, and that made it a big occasion for all of us. My father even gave me money to buy a new dress to wear. I found a lovely black one, a knitted sheath that fit me like a glove. I loved it and was anxious to show it off, but then I felt a wave of guilt at wanting to exhibit myself in it.

The evening of the party I dressed and applied makeup carefully and then looked myself over in the mirror in our bedroom. The jet black dress clung to my every curve, highlighting my burnished hair and the slash of red lipstick with which I'd outlined my lips. I really shouldn't wear this, I thought, it's too sexy, too clinging. Just then, Jack came into the room. He looked me over and gave a long low wolf whistle. "Boy, do you ever look terrific, lady! Whooee! You'll be the belle of the ball tonight in that dress, that's for sure." I giggled happily, and I looked at myself again in the mirror. It *was* a lovely dress, I conceded, and I was proud and happy that I looked so good in it. After all, tonight was my first chance in a long time to be out with my husband, and I wanted him to see me as an attractive date who he looked forward to taking home, not a tired mother of two. I picked up my coat, and we set out in high spirits.

Everyone was in a happy, laughing mood. Once, I caught Ron Larrinaga gazing hard at me. He stared openly, then gave me a look that seemed reproachful, or maybe I just imagined it. It was a look that made me uncomfortable, but he didn't come over and speak to me—he was busy witnessing to several others about his conversion. Janet was with him, wearing the same dress she had worn to church that first time, looking tired as ever, poor thing. I resolved to issue that invitation to lunch to her and the children. Shortly after that

I walked up to her and did. Ron accepted for them both. And having done my duty, I went back to mingling with our other friends. After about a half hour at each stop, we piled gaily into cars and drove in a caravan to the next place. It was a lot of fun, and soon I forgot about Ron Larrinaga.

At the third house, where the main course was served, there was a piano. After the meal, one of the men went over to it and began playing. We quickly gathered around to listen. I was one of the first ones there. Al played well, and, though I had avoided music and dancing in high school, I really loved good music, especially hymns and jazz. I was leaning against the piano, tapping my toe in time to the music, when Ron Larrinaga suddenly pushed through the group and stood next to me. Absorbed in Al's playing, I ignored him. Suddenly he spoke, loudly. "Music should only be used to glorify God, and those who play it for other reasons are not properly related to God." With that, he turned and walked away. We were all stunned. Al's hands fell away from the keys. There was a moment of uncomfortable silence. Then everyone moved guiltily away from the piano. The laughing carefree mood of the evening was shattered. We had all looked forward to this evening, and now this newcomer with his lofty attitude had spoiled it. I was annoyed with Ron, but then, I rationalized to myself, his spiritual basis for saying what he did is probably sounder than ours.

Jack, though, was in no mood for spiritual reasoning or rationalization. He was outraged. "Boy, what a royal pain that Ron is," he complained as we drove home. "Always acting so superior to everybody as if he had a direct line to God! 'Music should only be used to glorify God . . . '" he mimicked sarcastically. "What a jerk! Who the hell does he think he is anyway?"

"Jack!" I reproved sharply. "Mind your language!" Ron's words had raised an old conflict within me. As born-again Christians, we had been told to turn away from worldly temptations and devote ourselves instead to fellowship with other Christians with similar values, avoiding those who would lead us in another direction. But Ron's words had also raised rebellion in me. I had been having fun, and I resented him making me feel guilty about it. Now I wondered. "Well," I said, "maybe he shouldn't have said that, but then again, maybe he's right." Then I couldn't resist sniping, "Anyway, he's certainly shown that he's a lot more spiritual than you are. He's a good husband and father who pays close attention to his family's spiritual welfare. It's obvious he has stronger beliefs than you do." At that, anger tightened Jack's jaw, but he said nothing. It had been a thorn in my side ever since we got married that Jack was reluctant to commit his life as deeply to Christ as I wanted him to, and, though I had been instrumental in converting him, in convincing him to be born again, he wasn't terribly devout—certainly not in the way Ron Larrinaga was. I wanted us to be more like Ron and his family: dignified, God-fearing in all that we did, with well-behaved children like his, who showed complete respect for their father as head of the household. In my mind's eye, I pictured us like a Norman Rockwell painting—clean, well-scrubbed, happy, our heads bowed in perfect devotion over Sunday dinner. The evening, so happy to begin with, ended on a sour note, and though I had hoped for a romantic finale in my husband's arms, we went to bed not speaking.

The following Wednesday Ron and his family arrived for lunch at noon. Remembering how woebegone they

looked, I served a hot lunch of pot roast and mixed vegetables and then lemon cake and coffee, with milk for the little
ones. I used my wedding silver and china. After we ate, my
kids wanted to play in the backyard, in the sandbox Jack had
lovingly built for them. I invited the Larrinaga kids to go outdoors and play with them. Ron immediately intervened. "No.
They'll stay here with me. I prefer to have them where I can
keep an eye on them." I thought, What a good father he is!
He is so concerned about his children's safety and behavior.

Mine were miniature tornadoes, and I always had my
hands full with them. Jack couldn't help much, because of
school and work. He was rarely home, and, when he was, he
was studying or trying to sleep. So it fell to me to handle all
the domestic chores and the children. I wished that Jack
could take charge sometimes like Ron did and give me some
relief.

I didn't challenge Ron's decision about his children,
and they all stayed inside, sitting quietly at the table or on the
floor at their father's feet. They were extremely subdued and
quiet. I thought that was a bit strange since it's almost impossible for little children to keep quiet all the time, but the
Larrinaga children never uttered a word, nor did they move,
until their father gave them permission to do so. I admired
the way he kept them under such good control. I felt I had a
whole lot to learn from this man of God. I certainly didn't
know, that sunny afternoon, into what hell my innocent
desire to learn from Ron Larrinaga would lead us all.

That afternoon, as on the previous occasions we'd
met, Ron immediately took center stage, ignoring me, his
wife, and his children. Sitting at the head of the table, he
launched into a long and emotional recital, a more in-depth

history of himself than he had given us before. It was a solil-
oquy I would hear again and again in the years to come—so
often that it was burned indelibly into my brain. His family,
though they must have heard the story many times, sat as
though mesmerized, giving him their full attention.

"I was born in the Bronx," he began, as though reading from a script. "My mother's parents were Norwegian,
and my grandmother, my mother's mother, sang in the opera
and wrote poetry. My grandfather was an artist of great
renown and went to live with the Navajo Indians. He did the
historical artwork for the Santa Fe Railroad. My father was
part Mexican, born in Baja, California. He met and married
my mother, Solveig Gand, in New Jersey. They argued and
fought bitterly until they separated, when I was about three.
I was an only child." He paused to take a sip of coffee but did
not touch the cake I had put on his plate. "I was only five
when I found myself thrown out on the street during the day,
to fend for myself. I had to get on the buses and ride them
just to keep warm. Some days, the movie house manager
would let me stay in the theater, just so I could sit there all
day and stay warm and not die of exposure to the cold. I'd
crawl around on the floor, under the seats, and search for left-
over candy or popcorn to eat. I was always sick. I had
scarlet fever and tapeworms and all the worst childhood
diseases."

I found myself murmuring sympathetically at this sad
tale of his childhood. I ventured a question. "Where was your
mother during all this? Why didn't she take better care of
you?"

"My mother was working. It was the people she paid
to look after me who did that to me."

22

"Didn't you tell your mother what was happening?" I asked.

"Yes, but my parents didn't believe me. They believed the stories the others told them. I was afraid of my father. He was very violent. He would beat my mother over the head with my Christmas toys." I gasped in shock. "Then my mother got a tumor on the brain," he went on dolefully. "She loved me, but she was too sick to take care of me." At that point I got up and looked out the kitchen window anxiously just to be sure my kids were okay. They were happily digging in the sandbox.

"Would the kids like more milk, some more cake?" I asked Janet.

"No, they're fine," said Ron. He looked annoyed at the interruption. Janet didn't say a word. "Let's see, where was I?" he went on. "Oh, yes. When I was seven, I was put into an orphanage. My mother was dying. Whenever I went to see her, they had her in this bed with high bars all around it. It was terrifying to me to see her like that. I couldn't touch her, and she couldn't touch me. She promised me she'd get well, but she died of her tumor on Saint Patrick's Day." Tears welled up in his eyes, and his voice choked as he recounted his mother's death.

"After my mother died, I was put in the orphanage for good. It was supposed to be a Christian orphanage, but I was beaten with a chair leg by a man with red hair and fury in his beady little eyes. I was locked in a closet for hours in the dark. I had things stolen from me every day of my life while in that Home. I would go out back, into the woods, and cry for hours on end, grieving for my mother. The other kids sometimes found me there, and they would tie me to a tree, in the snow, and leave me there. I never knew if they were going to come back and let me go or not. Two of the bigger boys tried to get me to do unnatural acts with them, sins against God and Jesus Christ, unnatural acts!" Ron's voice rose passionately, and he seemed very agitated. I felt sorry for him. What a terrible childhood he'd had. "When I refused, they would grab my nose and twist it around until it was nothing but a mass of purple blood and bruises. And because I didn't submit to them, they'd hang me out the window, upside down, holding me only by one leg, and from the third floor! I thought I was going to die." He paused, out of breath.

I was absolutely horrified by his tale. What an awful childhood this poor man had had! It overwhelmed me that anyone could suffer such abuse and still have grown up to find Christ and deep love for God. He was amazing. I found myself admiring him even more.

Though he seemed anxious to continue his story, it was too horrific. I really didn't want to hear any more. I went outside to check on my children. When I returned with them, I glanced over at the Larrinaga kids. They looked sleepy. "The kids look a little tired," I said. "Why don't we let the little ones lie down in my room and have a nap, while we finish our coffee?"

"They're fine," said Ron. "They don't need a nap right now." My kids were already running around the room, trying to make friends with the others and interrupting to get my attention every time Ron tried to start his story up again. I excused myself again and went and put them down for a nap.

As soon as I returned to the table, Ron resumed his tale as though nothing had happened in the interim. I was concerned that his little ones had to sit there and hear such a terrifying story, but they had apparently heard it all before, many times. Ron got up from the table and paced restlessly up and down the room as he talked. He was very excited, caught up in the drama of his tale. "My father left me in that orphanage and only came to see me once in awhile. On one of his visits, when I was ten or eleven, I begged him to take me out of there. He said he'd see. Then he came back and said he couldn't. My grandmother wouldn't let me live with her, and he had to work and couldn't look after me. So I was left there. My grandmother came to see me once in a while, but she didn't get me out of there. When I was sixteen, I left. I stayed with my grandmother part of the year, in Teaneck, New Jersey, and with my father, who by then had moved to Hoboken, for part of the year. Sometimes I stayed with my aunt, my mother's sister."

One of the children coughed. Ron glared at the child, and it immediately was quiet. "Children need to be disciplined," he declared, turning to fix me with a look. "It's God's word." I wondered at that, given the tale he had just told of his own 'disciplined' childhood. But I accepted his parental authority, and said nothing. Like the others, I sat and listened quietly, even though it was difficult to sit through his long-winded recital.

"At seventeen," he went on, "I enlisted in the military service. I was attending Jet Fighter Mechanic School in Amarillo, Texas. I was looking forward to graduating and to going home with my buddies to New York on leave. I got behind a day with my schooling, so at the last, I couldn't go with them. The bus my buddies were on went off a cliff outside Oklahoma City, and they were all killed or badly hurt."

"Oh, what a shock that must have been for you," I interjected softly.

He agreed and said, "The Lord had spared my life. I began to contemplate the meaning of life and death. I had had the fear of God put into me, and I wanted to know my Creator, if one existed. I was afraid to die with all my sins and go to Hell. I thanked the Lord for sparing my life and not allowing me to die on that bus."

Just then, a weary Jack came in from work and quietly dropped his long, lean frame into a nearby chair. Pausing for a moment, Ron said hello to him and then went right on. "Up to the time of the accident," he continued, "my life had been profane. I, like my Savior, am a man of sorrows, and well acquainted with grief. It is written: 'When your mother and father forsake you, then the Lord will take you up and be to you a father, and ye shall be my son.'" His eyes raked us as though daring us to disagree. I saw Jack quirk an eyebrow, and I shot him a look, silently beseeching him to have patience. It was getting late in the afternoon, and I was sure Ron would soon conclude and they would leave, so I could get Jack his supper. But he went on. "I was transferred to Massachusetts, where I married my high school sweetheart." I thought it strange that he talked as though reading from a resume and referred to his wife Janet, who was sitting right there, in the third person. It was spooky that he didn't even look at her when he spoke her name. It was like he was doing some kind of recitation, and she wasn't really part of it. "We were only nineteen years old, and our first baby was still-born. It was a terrible tragedy to us, and we thought maybe we wouldn't have any more babies. But we didn't accept then that it was God who controlled our lives and not us."

Just then, my son Philip woke from his nap, and cried loudly. Jack and I both dashed to get the children. "When is he going to leave so I can have dinner and get to work?" Jack complained, as we each grabbed a child.

"Shh! They'll hear you. Soon, I hope," I whispered back. "He's been going on like this for hours! But he's had an awful life. Be nice. I'll tell you all about it later." We went back to the kitchen. My children immediately started running around, trying to get the other kids to play with them. Ron turned to me and looked at me sternly. "Your children are wild and untamed." I was flabbergasted. "You should strive to train them better," he remonstrated me. "They should learn to sit still and listen when an adult speaks. 'Spare the rod, spoil the child.' God expects us, as parents, to discipline them."

He then went on to tell us that terrible consequences would befall those undisciplined as children, and quoted extensively from the Old Testament, from Ecclesiastics, about the training and raising of children. By the time he finished, I was convinced I had somehow been an inept or inadequate parent to my two children, that I didn't really understand what God intended as my responsibility as a parent. Then, as though nothing had happened, he resumed his history. I held Philip tightly on my lap and shushed him sternly when he tried to wriggle away and go over to his Daddy. I was rewarded with a look of approval from Ron. He droned on, and we marveled at his ability to keep going for so long. Jack was getting fidgety, and I knew his patience was fast running out. He was hungry, and he needed to clean up and have a nap before going to work at the post office. He stood up and tried to slip away to the bedroom. "You should really stay and listen," said Ron. "God, the Holy Spirit, has motivated me to speak to you about these things. 'Those who are not for God are against Him,' and you need to decide where you stand."

Jack and I looked at each other, and Jack sat down again, sheepishly. We were both feeling guilty and ill at ease. I was worried that, between our unruly kids and my disinterested husband, we had offended God and the Larrinagas. We were confused not only by our guests' unusual behavior, but by our response to it. We felt very unsure of ourselves. Although I was fascinated by the man and admired the strength of his beliefs, nevertheless I found myself wishing they'd just leave and let me get back to the reality of taking care of my own family. I needed time to think and to feed my hungry, tired husband and my two children. I was sorry I had asked them to come and then I felt guilty at feeling this way.

After what seemed an eternity, they left. I breathed a sigh of relief as I watched from the window as their car disappeared down the road. Hastily, I fed Jack, and he went off to work. I fell into bed exhausted and had troubled dreams.

The next night, at supper, Jack and I talked about the Larrinagas and their strange visit. We tried to figure out what it was about Ron that bothered us so much. We liked him, and we didn't like him. "He makes me feel like we don't measure up," I said. "We don't seem to have the devotion to God that we should."

"Well, he sure seems to think he has it, and can show us the way," said Jack resentfully, "but he's really a dedicated and zealous Christian and seems sincere in his beliefs. I don't know, maybe he has something to tell us. But he sure says a lot while he's doing it," Jack observed.

"Do you think he means it, about being sent by God?" I wondered aloud. "Maybe we don't have proper concern for God's will, like he said."

"Who knows?" said Jack tiredly. "I do the best I can. Right now, I just have to get through another night at work. I can't worry about God, I have to make a living so we can have a roof over our heads. You handle it."

I sighed. That was the way things usually ended. "You handle it," Jack would say and go on to school or work. I thought about the way Ron had spoken to me about my need to bring my family closer to God's will. He accompanied his admonitions and suggestions with appropriate quotations from Scripture, all of which just rolled off his tongue, and all of which reinforced his position. There was no rebuttal to God's word. I felt chastened and unworthy. He made me feel small and insignificant next to the depth and power of his knowledge and devotion. I wished we had his discipline, his intelligence. Not that we weren't intelligent, but we certainly didn't have anywhere near the Scriptural knowledge Ron did. I envied this in him. I began studying my Bible more.

In the weeks that followed, Ron and his family often dropped in on me in the afternoon. Once in a while, Ron would stop by alone. On these occasions, he was always careful to take me outside, and we'd stand there while he talked. "Why are we standing out here?" I asked him the first time.

"Because I don't want the neighbors to talk," he said. I didn't know what he meant. "I don't want them to think there is anything lascivious going on if we're here alone."

That surprised me. We didn't have any neighbors nearby, and, anyway, it would never have occurred to me. But I didn't challenge him, and we'd stand there uncomfortably in the afternoon heat while he delivered his oratory. At least the children were able to play outdoors while we spoke. His exhortation to put away our faithless ways continued to make me feel guilty and unworthy, and I resolved to try harder to please him, and God.

Gradually, insidiously, as I struggled to find the spiritual perfection of which I had always dreamed, Ron cemented his hold on me. "I can see the Holy Spirit working in your heart," he'd say. I'd brighten. He'd center his attention on me, praising me that at last I was learning to submit to God's will. I'd flush with pleasure on hearing that. Then he'd contrast my newly achieved submission with Jack's failure to do the same. Jack, it seemed, was stubbornly resisting Ron's attempts to bring him to deeper obedience and devotion to God's will. Ron's rare praise made me even more determined to increase my commitment and my submission, and get Jack to submit too, because, as Ron quoted frequently, "'It is through the wife that an unbelieving husband is reached.'"

"If you love your husband, you must submit to God's word," was his constant admonishment, "and you must help your husband to submit." It was up to me. I was pleased that I was finally doing the right thing for God, not realizing we were falling into a web of evil. I worked on Jack relentlessly.

Ron Larrinaga and his family came to our house more and more often. As time went on, he zeroed in on my spiritual needs. I don't know if I was emanating waves that he sensed, or if he acted similarly with others. I certainly didn't suspect that he was carefully baiting a trap: I didn't see or smell the bait. Jack was working on studying and, aside from resenting Ron's growing presence, he didn't pay much attention to what was happening. He didn't notice Ron's influence over me extending to control.

"Why do they have to be here all the time, and him endlessly preaching, when I come home from school?" Jack complained testily. "Doesn't he know I have to have dinner and get to work? Doesn't he ever work?" I'd wondered about that, too. Ron had only occasional, part-time jobs. I wondered how they earned enough on which to live.

Nevertheless, I dismissed Jack's complaints as childish and listened to Ron Larrinaga's long-winded sermons attentively. I soaked up his exhortations to be a more devoted Christian. I continued studying my Bible daily, and I prayed to God to help me follow Ron and, through him, learn how better to obey God's will for me. "I am the chosen servant of Jesus Christ," Ron declared again and again, "sent by God to minister to you and teach you His will for you."

I believed him wholeheartedly. I wanted to believe him. Ron Larrinaga, to my naive eyes and hungry spirit, exemplified the Christian beliefs I so desperately desired for my family. Moreover, I pressed Jack to listen with me, and, since he knew how much I wanted our family to exemplify Christian life and underneath wanted it himself, he gradually stopped objecting and began listening to Ron also. Before many more months had passed, we were beyond reason, almost completely in Ron Larrinaga's cult-like thrall.

I led the way. I ignored all warnings and rushed heedlessly down the wrong path into Ron Larrinaga's clutches. Worse, I dragged my husband and children along with me.

2

sting of the serpent

We began pushing out of our lives not only our church, whose beliefs Ron assured us were "at odds with God's word," but our families and those of our friends who didn't accept Ron or his faith. We started cutting ourselves and our children off from them and steadfastly resisted their interference.

By the time Jack graduated from college we were already heavily under Ron Larrinaga's influence. He convinced us that Jack should use his new degree to teach only in a Christian school. "You can throw your God-given talent away on a teaching job in a secular school," he said, "or start right now to serve God and bend to His will for you by going on to study the Bible and teach His word. I, as his chosen servant, know that this is what God wants you to do." That was a very attractive idea to us, especially to me. It was right in line with what I wanted for our family. Jack would be teaching God's word every day, to Christian children, and we would be serving God as He intended us to do, according to Ron.

"Why don't we all go to Arizona?" Ron suggested casually. "Jack and I will enroll in the a Bible college together, and when we finish, we will both teach in Christian schools."

"Oh, what a wonderful idea!" I was thrilled. "Let's do it, Jack!" I wanted us to go but Jack wasn't all that keen on it. I nagged him and worked on him every day to agree to do it. We discussed it briefly with our families, but they were dead set against it. They didn't want us to leave California, especially not with the Larrinagas.

"Why can't Jack get a teaching job here, near your home?" my mother wanted to know.

"You know, Mary, that guy Ron has too much influence over you. You don't know anything about him, really, but you're willing to traipse off at the first word from him," my sister warned. But I was adamant. Ron was the road to our Christian salvation, of that I was sure. I kept working on Jack, and finally he gave in and agreed we'd go to Arizona. I was overjoyed. Our spiritual and secular lives were at last going to converge on the course I had envisioned for us of a devout family, spending our days serving God.

My father was furious. My parents had little use for Ron Larrinaga and his, as they called them, "fanatical beliefs," and were deeply upset about the influence he exerted over me, our lives, and our decisions.

Dad reacted angrily to my continual "Ron says this" and "Ron believes that." Ron by then had become not only my spiritual mentor, but my ideal, perhaps even my idol. I was very attracted to him and his beliefs.

Dad finally blew up at me one day at a family gathering. "Ron!" he exclaimed. "That's all I ever hear from you anymore, Mary. What's gotten into you? I don't like him, and I don't like the way you're letting him influence you and tell you what to do! There's too damned much gobbledygook from that man, and I don't believe him or trust him for a minute! He's nothing but a leech, and he's going to mess your lives up. Don't you and Jack think for yourselves any more?"

My sister Marilyn, too, joined in. "You're really going too far with this thing, Mary," she said. I could tell she was mad at me, but I didn't really care. Only Ron mattered. "You've got Mom and Dad all upset, and you keep shutting me out, too. We don't know what to do any more to make you see reason because you're so taken with this man. I feel like I'm losing my little sister and my niece and nephew. Mom and Dad are really upset, Mary, and you should think about them for a change, and the rest of your family, not just yourself and this . . . this Ron!" She said his name like an epithet.

A pang of remorse stung me seeing how upset they all were, especially my father. However, my new found resolve to live my faith overcame such feelings. "None of you ever understood my spirituality, or my need to devote my life to serving Christ!" I retorted. How could they understand why I wanted to follow Ron, whose life was devoted to serving God, more than I wanted to be with them? "Anyway, Marilyn, you and the boys have no room to complain. You certainly can't brag about your religious devotion when you seldom even go to church!" With that parting shot, I slammed out angrily and didn't go back.

Jack's family, too, tried to dissuade us. "It's just self-ishness by all of them, wanting us here near them more than concern for our spiritual welfare," I told Jack when he expressed concern about leaving our families. Meanwhile, Ron was always there, always friendly and reassuring, always gently countering my doubts with Scriptural reassurances, which I would then parrot to Jack. Ron encouraged us to ignore our families and not listen to them.

"You must realize they are influenced by Satan more than by God and do not understand the will of God for your lives. You must not let them turn you from the path to salvation," he insisted.

In the end, my need for religion, compulsive by then, caused us to cut our ties with our families and headed for Arizona with the Larrinagas. My spirit was high.

I was especially proud that I had convinced my husband to go and had visions of a grand and beautiful future. Jack would become as knowledgeable about Scripture as Ron. He would teach others. We would devote our lives and our family to the glory of God. What a wonderful life it would be! Achieving religious perfection in the eyes of God was my burning goal. I sang hymns in the car that first morning as we drove across the desert toward Arizona. But my zealous joy, and my utopian vision of the future, were short-lived.

By the second day on the road I was no longer singing. The trip had become a nightmare of cranky children, car trouble, and penny pinching, since we were paying the Larrinaga's expenses, too. Ron, it seemed, was broke. He never worked a full time job, since he had to "devote my days to the Lord." The Larrinagas by then had five children—Tommy had been born in California. We still had only two. We were poor, but they were poorer. We arrived in Phoenix and rented tiny duplex apartments. I had never been

anywhere so hot in my life. Ron got a part-time job as a
delivery man at night, and Jack turned to his former employ-
er, the Postal Service. It meant he had to work nights again,
but we needed the income and had little choice.

As soon as he had us away from familiar territory,
away from our homes and families, Ron's friendly tactics
changed. He began to browbeat both of us nonstop, questioning our devotion to God at every turn. "We can change
your rebellious ways only when you are willing to be willing
to submit to the Lord," he said to me sternly. He accused me
daily of having a poor attitude, of not standing behind my
husband's decision to serve the Lord, and of not giving both
of them my full support. "You are more interested in material things! Stop complaining about petty matters. You need to
look more to your spiritual well-being." I was shocked and
surprised by this change in the man I admired, and I was
upset that he felt I was not bending to God's will. I thought I
was doing that. Ron made me feel guilty and unworthy. I
worked harder to please him and never complained about
anything. Then he began to take me to task for my behavior
as a wife to Jack. I was too independent, too outspoken, he
declared. "A good wife is obedient to her husband's wishes
and bends her will to serve him, and God," he rebuked me
again and again. He began to demand that Jack take a stern-
er stance with me, and I felt Jack obediently began berating
me and belittling me. My self-assurance and self-esteem
plummeted.

I began to fear both of them. In my desire to show
myself worthy of their regard, especially of Ron's, I hastened
to obey whenever they demanded anything of me. I was

determined to be a good and supportive wife to Jack and a good Christian woman so I could please God and Ron Larrinaga, His chosen servant. I was so caught up in doing that, it didn't occur to me that there might be something wrong in the way I needed their approval, needed to submit to them. I didn't measure what pleasing them was exacting from me and what getting their approval was starting to require of me. I had only this mental image of a loving, devoted wife before me. Janet seemed to illustrate it, and I strove to be more like her, acquiescent, quiet and uncomplaining, obedient to Ron's every wish.

I felt Jack followed his lead, as Ron adopted an even sharper, more demanding attitude toward me as the weeks passed. They alternated contempt and command in speaking to me. Before long, I was being ordered around like a slave. If I objected, or complained about anything, I was severely rebuked. "You are a willful woman who is unwilling to bend to God. Stop worrying about fleshly things!" Ron would say, contempt dripping from his voice. "Get your mind on your spiritual failings instead. There's plenty to concern you there. You are a shallow, heedless person, unwilling to bend to God's will for you. Go to your room and pray for God to give you submissiveness."

The more they ordered, scolded, and rebuked me, the more I scurried around trying to please them, trying to be a model Christian wife, trying to comply with what they told me were "Biblical dictates for a good Christian wife." But nothing I did pleased them. Soon, I was miserable and unhappy.

I caught Ron looking at me speculatively on several occasions and wondered guiltily what I was doing wrong.

Somehow, his look always made me feel a sense of shame. Once, at their place, I was leaning into the car, lifting Louise out, and Ron came out to get the bag of groceries I had brought. "You have a good strong young body, Mary," he remarked suddenly from behind me. "You should not be so overly modest. Your skirts are much too long. We are your family. You do not need such modesty before us." I turned, with Louise in my arms, surprised at such a remark, and realized he must have been staring at my bare legs when I bent over to pick her up. However, I flushed with pleasure at that strange compliment, happy that there was something, anything about me, that he liked.

A few weeks later when we were at a park with the kids while our husbands were at Bible school, I told Janet I was unhappy about how Jack and Ron were acting toward me. She seemed neither surprised nor shocked. "That is the way of husbands," she said mildly. "We have to learn to submit ourselves to their will." With that, she raised her arm and showed me three ugly bruises on the soft area of her underarm. I gasped.

"Ron did that to you?" I asked. She nodded, but said nothing about how it had happened.

"A woman must obey her husband, and God's will for her," was all she would say.

One Sunday, when we were visiting them, they had Amy, a frail little child of fifteen months, confined in her high chair for hours while Ron went on and on with one of his lengthy oratories. After awhile, Amy became restless and began to fuss. To my surprise, Janet immediately snatched her roughly out of the high chair, took Amy into the next room and spanked her soundly with the back of a hairbrush until she was screaming and crying. Then she brought her back into the kitchen and plopped her down into the high chair again. "Now, sit there and be quiet," she commanded. At a harsh look from Ron, the child's sobs subsided in fear. But soon she was fussing and squirming again. Janet yanked her out of the high chair and took her into the bedroom again. I was horrified. I could hear the sharp smack of the hairbrush against bare flesh and the child's shrieks and screams of pain.

"Ow! Oh! No! I good, Mama! No!" Amy cried piteously, but the beating went on and on. Then, mercifully it stopped. Janet came out again without the child, slamming the door, shutting Amy in the bedroom by herself. We could hear her piteous sobbing from behind the closed door. Ron paid little attention to the scene and showed no emotion whatsoever, nor did the other children.

That stunned me. I felt ill and faint, but I didn't dare say anything. However, my face must have reflected my feelings, because Ron glared at me the way he had glared at Amy when she cried, a look that said clearly he'd relish beating me the same way Janet had just beaten their unruly child. "The rod and reproof give wisdom," he quoted solemnly. "Correct thy child and he shall give thee rest. He that rebuketh a man shall find more favor afterwards than he that flattereth with the tongue." He quoted from Proverbs, staring directly at me, and I felt deeply shamed that I had dared to question his actions in correcting his daughter. But, after that, I started making excuses not to go there when Jack went over for Bible study with Ron. I didn't want to be exposed to their discipline of their children anymore, and Ron's behavior toward me was making me decidedly uncomfortable.

We had been there barely three months when Ron declared he was completely dissatisfied with the Bible Institute. "They compromise with Scriptural doctrine," he declared. We didn't know then what a repetitive refrain that was. He would come to use it against every school, every teacher, every church, and every authority we encountered. But this was the first time we'd heard it, and we believed everything he said. He complained about the Institute daily, and it wasn't much longer before Ron abruptly quit, then talked Jack into quitting, too. "We'll do daily Bible study together at my place," said Ron. "I understand Scriptural doctrine much better than they do, and I don't compromise it."

By then, Ron wasn't even working part-time. "I cannot work for employers who demand that I compromise my beliefs and deviate from following the word and the will of God," he declared. Soon he was earning nothing and began "borrowing" from us. "It is your Christian duty to aid my ministry during this time of temporary need," he told us. We began trying to support both families on what little Jack earned at his part-time job. That arrangement quickly meshed our lives firmly with theirs. We maintained our own apartment but found we were spending most of our time over at their place. Jack studied every day with Ron, and our finances made it obligatory that we share shopping and meals.

We hadn't become acquainted with any other people , not even from the Bible college. Ron had demanded that all Jack's spare time be spent in Bible study with him, and I was too busy with the children, with helping Janet, and with trying to please Jack and Ron to try to make any new friends.

We heard nothing from our families who, unsympathetic and weary, had given up on us. So now, the Larrinagas were not only our only social contact, they became our substitute family, too.

After we'd been in Phoenix about a year, I became pregnant with our third child. We were scraping by on Jack's income, but barely. I was getting worried about how much longer we could manage supporting the Larrinagas and ourselves and was anxious for Jack to get a full time teaching job at a Christian school, as was our goal. Then Ron suddenly decided to move his family to an old house fifteen miles out of town. We were surprised that he wanted to move so far out, since it was so much more convenient to live in town. We didn't know then that his being distant from town and neighbors was important. For a period, we saw less of them after they moved out there. We couldn't afford the gas to visit them very often. Ron would come to town to go shopping with me and get groceries and take them back home. So we didn't really notice what was happening to June, their oldest child.

Ron's children were in public school, but he was extremely rigid and strict about what they could and could not do at school. "The children must learn to monitor each other while they are out among the heathen," he said to us. I asked Jack, since he was over at Ron's more than I was any more, what that meant, and he told me he was as puzzled about it as me.

Every evening, on returning from school, each of the Larrinaga children had to report to Ron everything, and he meant absolutely everything, that the other children had done or said at school, especially the other Larrinaga children.

Basically, they were being taught to squeal on each other. Then Ron would ruminate over it all, give lengthy discourses, consult his Bible, and mete out punishment to his kids—often beatings, or long confinement to their rooms, or deprivation of meals—for each infraction of prescribed behavior.

June, we knew, needed and wanted to be accepted at school. She was therefore being "monitored" very closely by her brothers, and it seemed that every day she did something wrong at school that merited severe punishment by Ron. "She's a willful child, who will take every opportunity to associate with the unsaved," he said. Everyone in the Larrinaga household, I later observed, was required to watch, spy upon, and report on everyone else. I thought that was pretty strange. Every move, every action, every word was analyzed by Ron, criticized, rewarded, or punished, in his words, "according to the will of God."

One day we heard Ron tell little June, "You are absolutely forbidden, do you hear, forbidden, to play with any of the other children at school, or to talk to any of them at recess! You will sit by yourself during recess! You will not mingle with the unsaved! Do you understand me?" The child, looking terrified, nodded silently. The only activity Ron approved for her, I learned, was supervised physical education class, where she had little or no opportunity to talk to other children. If she disobeyed in the slightest and Ron found out about it, he would strip her naked, take off his belt, and spank her soundly. One day when he had made Janet beat her in the bathroom, he paraded all the other children in to mock her as she stood naked and terrified inside the tub. It was no mild spanking, either. June was beaten until she had red welts and deep purple bruises on her backside and her legs. Once, when I happened to notice angry red welts on her legs, I protested to Ron.

"You're hitting June too much, Ron," I said. "You're liable to hurt her seriously if you don't go easier on her."

He turned to me in fury, spitting out Biblical quotations. "How dare you question me in God's will for my child?" he yelled. "A child left to himself bringeth his mother shame," he said scathingly, "and your children would be far better behaved if you administered more physical discipline! 'Withhold not correction from the child, for if thou beatest him with the rod, he shall not die. Thou shalt beat him with the rod and shalt deliver his soul from hell.'" I turned away, chastened, humiliated again by my Scriptural stupidity.

Then I noticed that whenever we went to visit them, June was not at the table with the rest of us. "Where's June?" I'd ask.

"She's being disciplined," Ron would reply coldly. "She's been rebellious, and she's getting no dinner tonight. She must remain alone to think about her transgressions. She is a willful, disobedient child, doing everything to oppose God's will for her. She will stay in her room, away from everyone else." Poor June, I thought. I wished she would be less willful, so she would be with us again. Little did I know.

When our baby Marian was born, I became totally occupied with her and with my own family. One day, Janet told us Ron was embroiled in a battle with the Phoenix school authorities and June's teachers. That worried me. Later, Jack asked him about what was going on. "She is to have nothing to do with the other children and accept nothing from those godless, unsaved teachers," said Ron. "I've told the school authorities I insist on going along on any field trips June has to take. I have a right to properly supervise my daughter, I told them, and to be sure she does not speak with any of the unsaved, and that our religious freedom is not being compromised on these trips. It is my constitutional right to be assured that nothing Godless occurs on those trips to taint my child."

"What did they say to that?" Jack wanted to know.

"Well, they didn't like it, but I'm going to insist on it," said Ron.

Poor skinny, dark-eyed little June, who never meant anyone any harm, continued being beaten almost daily when she came home from school. She was always doing something to offend God, in Ron's eyes. Occasionally, when I was there and saw her, she'd look at me with a sad, bewildered expression, saying nothing, not understanding what she had done that her very existence offended the eyes of God, as her father often told her. If Bobby, the next youngest child, failed to report to Ron's satisfaction on his sister June, he, too, was beaten severely with a belt, and the same happened to Randall if he didn't report on the other two.

At this point, Jack and I were repelled by Ron's ideas of child rearing, but Jack told me we should mind our own business. However, I couldn't ignore it any longer. Finally, I spoke up. "I think you're being much too hard on those kids, Ron. You shouldn't hit them so much, or so hard. They have to have some freedom at school, to grow up like normal kids. As it is, they're afraid to breathe, for fear you'll give them a licking." I immediately regretted having spoken.

Ron jumped to his feet and turned on me in a rage like I'd never seen before. He put his face up close to mine, and

I could feel his hot breath as he yelled at me, veins standing out on his neck. I backed away in terror. "You! You dare to talk, you wicked, rebellious woman! You are a poor parent to your own children! You refuse to bend to God's will for you. Your very existence offends Him, too, and you should be taught obedience, as you have not been!"

Seeing his distorted face and wild eyes, I was even more terrified. I could see the children's fearful faces, too. Suddenly a wave of revulsion for this man engulfed me. I had to get away. I stormed out and didn't go back for several days, though Jack continued going for Bible study. "I told you you should mind your own business," Jack scolded me. "What they do with their kids is their business, and we don't have any right to interfere."

Then one day he came home completely disgusted, too. "I think Ron's going completely overboard with his kids," he said. "He has so many rules for them to follow that the poor kids can't escape doing something wrong that brings punishment down on them. I don't know, Mare," he said with deep concern in his voice, "maybe we need to distance ourselves from them for a while."

I agreed. "I don't like it, either," I confessed. "Poor little June is nothing but skin and bones, and she looks terrified all the time. So do Johnny and Randall. And they even spank the little one all the time. I can't stand to see it."

Somehow, Ron sensed our thoughts. The next afternoon he was at my door. Jack had taken Philip and Louise to the store with him, and baby Marian was sleeping. I had been enjoying my few minutes of peace, and I really resented Ron interrupting it. "Why didn't Jack come for Bible study today?" he wanted to know as soon as I answered the door.

The last thing I wanted was a confrontation with Ron about the Bible.

"Well," I said evasively, "Jack and I need some time to ourselves, Ron." I told him, "We're spending too much time with you lately. We need to be here in our own home, spending time as a family, together with our children. I need some peace and rest. The children are wearing me out, and, with studying and working, Jack is pretty tired of everything, too."

"Aha! I knew it! You are being rebellious against the will of God," said Ron. "You will be punished for it, you'll see. God will bring retribution down on your heads. We came to Phoenix to do the will of God, and now you are abandoning that for selfish pursuits! You are both rebellious!"

"I know that." I was immediately put on the defensive again. Ron's accusation of rebelliousness stung me, as it always did. "But we need to find our own way in serving God. Jack and I will continue to do the will of God for us, but right now we need some time to ourselves."

"Yourselves! You see how selfish and self-centered you are? Rebellion," he fixed me with a glare, "is the same as witchcraft! It will be punished severely by God." At my shocked look, he launched into more quotations from Scripture.

Once started, he didn't stop for over an hour. He stood on my front doorstep and berated me, accusing me of "totally abandoning God and influencing your husband to do the same." He told me how selfish and unconcerned with God I was. I stood there trembling, trapped and ashamed, unable to slam the door in his face. Finally, he turned and stormed back to his car and drove away. His diatribes always left me trembling, filled with fear and guilt. Afterward, I couldn't eat or sleep, and I felt depressed and discouraged. I was also beginning to realize that I feared Ron, as one fears a jailer in authority. Jack and I weren't in control of our lives any more—Ron Larrinaga was.

The next day, Ron came to our house again. This time he found Jack home, and he promptly ignored me and began working on Jack as he had me the day before. "You are to blame for your wife's irresponsible ways," he said angrily. "Her failure to submit to God's will is your fault. You are too lenient with her. God's word tells you it is your responsibility as a husband and father and head of the family as God has ordained it, to bring your wife around and make her obey. It's the wife's duty to submit to her husband! As Christ is the head of the Church, so is the husband the head of the home, and the wife must submit to his will as to God's," he said. Jack nodded throughout the tirade. I felt he agreed completely with Ron, since he didn't say anything. Ron raved on. Neither of us was smart enough or well enough versed in Scripture to dispute Ron or answer his accusations with Scriptural proof for our own position. He always had a better answer and three quotes from Scripture to back it up.

Ron's attitude changes during that period were so extreme, so radical, that I was continually whipsawed back and forth in how I felt about him. He'd shout at us angrily and berate us, and we'd get mad and leave. Quickly, he'd switch behavior and become charming, loving, and soft-spoken.

We weren't physicians or psychologists, and we didn't recognize the signs that Ron Larrinaga was a man who was seriously mentally deranged. I believed his mood swings were signs of God at work within him, as he assured us they were. Within the week, that time, his attitude toward us changed, and, as always, I forgave and forgot. Life resumed as before, and Jack returned to his Bible study at Ron's.

After a while, the fact that June wasn't around when we visited, that she was always "being disciplined and thinking about her transgressions" went almost unnoticed.

It wasn't long before Ron made his next move on us. First, he confronted Jack. Jack's part-time postal job required him to deliver the mail to a few bars along his route. "Isaiah says that the servant of God shall not occupy his hands in doing evil, and it is evil and wicked of you to deliver mail to a bar. God will surely punish you, and all of us, for your transgression in this! To atone for your sins and to prove you love God, you must leave that job at once!"

I was shocked. Jack's job at the post office was supporting us all, however meagerly. "But, Ron, surely you don't mean that. Jack's job is the only money we get. It's all we have to support us all, your family included."

"I do mean it," he insisted. "You must show your faith in God's will for you by quitting that job at once!" He kept up his campaign along those lines for a week, without cease. The following week, feeling challenged to prove his devotion to God's work, Jack quit his job.

I was stunned and scared. "How are we going to manage, or pay our bills?" Somehow Ron was able to get Jack to do it to me. It was a measure of how far Jack had now fallen under his spell.

"God will provide," Ron assured us with great confidence. We waited for that to happen. Soon we couldn't pay our bills. We were nearly out of food, and I began to panic. "Ye of little faith! You must trust in the Lord," Ron rebuked me angrily, "and open your heart to Him, in order to receive His help." He turned to Jack. "In this time of great need, we would do better in God's eyes to gather together and combine our resources for the good of all, for only then will He send help to us, when we are waiting His will together in this. You must move in with us now," he said, "so we can spend our time praying diligently together. God will soon hear us and send us new resources as we spend our days in waiting upon the Lord."

Obediently, we moved out to their remote neighborhood to join forces with them in waiting upon the Lord for help. Fortunately, we didn't notify our landlord or break the lease on our apartment. I hated that old house of theirs so far out of town, but we told ourselves that we had no choice. Soon, with all those mouths to feed, what little money and food Jack and I had left were gone. Our meals for several days were sparse and intermittent, and the children began to cry from hunger. Ron and Janet silenced their children with angry rebuke and frequent beatings with a strap or hairbrush. I was horrified at that. "If you don't stop that, we're going to leave and go home to our own apartment," I warned. I kept my own children protectively close to me.

"You are willful and sinful and unwilling to wait upon God's will for you! Open your heart and mind to His will, and, you will see, God will provide." This time, having staked all on Ron's say-so, Jack had to side with him. So we stayed there and waited upon the Lord to provide for us, but my heart beat in fear for my children and our survival. We were all hungry. Our stomachs were growling constantly, and there was no money for food, let alone anything else. Janet was pregnant again, and I was worried about her. She looked so pale and weak.

Once in a while, Ron received a small check from his father, who was living somewhere back east. "Guilt money," he usually called it. But he never sent the checks back. "I will use this money for my ministry," he always said. Ron now decided that God would move his father to send another check. We prayed and waited impatiently each day for the mailman to pass, but no check arrived.

Then a day came that we had only some baby cereal and a few onions left in the house. We peeled the onions and boiled them in a huge pot of water, adding salt and Worcestershire sauce to give the broth some taste. That was what the grown-ups and older children ate for several days. Then that, too, was gone.

Marian was about seven months old, and I wasn't nursing her any more. I mixed the dry baby cereal with water and spooned it into her. She cried and howled hungrily for more. It was the last meal she'd get unless we somehow got some money to buy food. I started to cry and turned to Jack. "You have to go somewhere, anywhere, and get us help! We need food for the baby and the children." I turned to Ron. "Janet needs food in her condition. You can't do this." He ignored me. Desperate, I screamed, "Please, you have to stop this! There is no check coming! God isn't hearing us! You must go and get us some food somehow! We'll all starve. The children are getting sick. They'll die!"

"Ye of little faith!" Ron glared at me. "How dare you question us, woman, and God's will for you! He will never hear your prayers, rebellious woman!" Then he launched into a tirade against me as I sat there, sobbing in fright and despair. To my horror, Jack chimed in and began berating me, too, backing Ron up.

"You are a foolish, willful woman," he said, "and I am your husband and head of your home. You will obey me, do you hear?" Ron nodded approvingly at that. I looked up at both of them, and suddenly I was very terrified, for myself and for my children. But I quelled my rebellion and kept quiet, praying to God to forgive me for my outburst and my lack of faith.

Another day went by during which we ate nothing. We read Scriptures that would comfort us and give us hope. Jack and I talked to each other and encouraged each other, each trying to shore up the other's faith as we weakened. The children were now crying and whining from hunger all the time, and Marian screamed constantly, shrieking even louder in outrage when I offered her only water to suck from her bottles.

To my deluded mind, with Ron constantly exhorting us to greater faith and greater trust in God, it became a test of my faith in the Lord, of our willingness, as Ron put it, to submit our lives to God, to wait upon His will for us. I was determined this time not to cave in. I wanted desperately to prove to Ron that we believed God would rescue us from starvation. Mercifully, He did. Probably from physical deprivation and hunger, Janet went into premature labor that night.

Edward, their sixth baby, was born the following morning. Janet was, of course, given full meals at the hospital. She sent most of her food and all the milk they allowed her home to us. I'd divide what little it was among the eight kids at home, giving Marian two bottles a day of watered milk and a few spoonfuls of mashed potato to soothe her. When Ron brought us the food—a small carton of milk, a sandwich, a plate with a little meat and potatoes on it—we'd fall on our knees to give thanks to God for providing for us. Then I'd divide it and parcel it out, a swallow of milk, a bit of food for each. It barely helped. The kids still cried piteously from hunger, but some food had miraculously, according to Ron, appeared. "God has shown us His infinite mercy," he declared. "God has provided! Get on your knees, all of you, and beg His forgiveness for doubting Him, for not completely submitting your will to His!"

When Janet and the baby were released from the hospital after four days, the supply line closed. She was home, and we had two more mouths to feed. I prayed earnestly to God hourly not to let Janet's milk dry up. Compassionately, each time she nursed tiny Edward, she pumped her breast to squeeze out some milk into a glass for Marian's bottles.

By then none of us could function well, we were so physically weakened from hunger. The children no longer played. They just whined, "I'm hungry, Mommy," or, "My stomach hurts." When Ron's kids complained, he'd take them into the next room and beat them, demanding that they "submit their will to God without complaint." They were too weak to even cry when he whaled into them. Finally, when he began to beat little Amy again for crying from hunger, I snapped.

I jumped up and grabbed his arm to stop him. "Stop that this minute!" I screamed. "What kind of father are you? What kind of a man? Your family is starving. My family is starving. Do something, do you hear me? You have to do something to get food for these children. They can't live like this!" I turned to Jack, crying and yelling. "You too! Stop this right now! You're both crazy! Our children will die if we keep this up, and it will be YOUR fault, not God's!"

I became a wild woman, and even Ron saw that he couldn't move me. He grumbled and bitterly rebuked me, but gave in when I wouldn't be quelled. Within the hour, he and Jack went out to go to the free government surplus warehouse in Phoenix. They brought back flour, sugar, peanut butter, a couple of loaves of bread, two small cans of stew meat, lettuce, and some half-rotted squash. When I saw the food, even though I knew it wouldn't last very long with so many of us to feed, my hands shook and tears streamed down my face. I put together the first meal we had seen in weeks. Ron insisted that "Before we take a bite of this food we will give thanks to God for rescuing us from starvation!" Then he proceeded to say thanks to God for what seemed like hours before we could eat. We fell on our food like a pack of animals. None of us would cognize that God hadn't "saved us" from starvation. We didn't need to starve. We had brought starvation on ourselves, by our own foolish actions.

After we had eaten, Ron turned on me. "You!" he snarled. "You are more interested in food for your belly than in serving God!" I was then subjected to a two-hour harangue. "You have a poor attitude and are preoccupied with fleshly matters! You have an abnormal concern for personal modesty and are trying to isolate yourself and your family from God's will for you." That attack was the last straw. Personal modesty indeed. Slim to begin with, I had lost an alarming amount of weight since Marian's birth, especially in these past couple of weeks, and my physical condi-

tion was poor. I had been forced to listen to children screaming and crying from hunger or senseless beatings, day and
night, for weeks. I thought I had been strong, that I had followed Ron's dictates and put my faith totally in God.

I jumped up from where I was sitting. "Shut up!" I
shrieked. "I don't want to hear any more from you! I don't
care what you think! This is crazy! Nothing we do or say is
right with you! I'm through trying to please you, or please
God the way you want us to. We're leaving." Then I turned
to Jack. "You must believe my true spirit and give me support in this," I pleaded, "for our children's sake." Then I
turned back to Ron. "I am leaving here, with or without my
husband, and I'm taking my children with me. I'm not going
to put up with you and your constant criticism any more. And
we're not going to starve just to please you! I don't think
that's what God wants, I think it's what YOU want!"

I had never dared to speak to either Ron or Jack like
that before, and I didn't know what would happen, but I
knew I had to get out of there with my children, and I knew
it was urgent. I shouted almost hysterically at Jack, "We're
getting out of here, do you hear me? We're not staying another
minute! We're going back to our own apartment, with our
own family!" Without a word, he began gathering up our
things while I went to get the children. He didn't argue with
me, or take Ron's side. I was glad that he was ready to go,
too.

On the ride back to our apartment, I prayed to God that
the landlord wouldn't have noticed we were gone, and that
Jack could get his job back. The apartment was still waiting,
but the job wasn't. They advised us to check with the unem-
ployment office to see if we had eligibility. To our great

relief, we did. We survived on food from government surplus until the first check came, and then we were able to catch up on our rent and utilities. Jack studied the Bible at home and went out looking for jobs. I heaved a sigh of relief, though deep down I was confused and depressed.

3

caught in the snares

Two weeks later, Ron showed up. He rang the bell and banged on the door, but I refused to open the door or talk to him, so he stood outside, shouting through the closed door at me, where everyone in the neighborhood could hear him. "You've turned against God!" he bellowed. "You deserted us and left us to die! What kind of Christians are you? How can you claim to honor God with your selfish attitude? It is wicked, do you hear? God will judge you, you will see. He will judge you as He does all wickedness and all sinners! You will be severely rebuked by God for giving in to Satan and your temporal, fleshly desires."

I didn't know what to do or how to handle him. What would people who heard him think of me? I knew I should keep silent, but his accusations about being a bad Christian and abandoning Janet and the baby stung me into replying. "That's not true!" I yelled back through the door. "We believed God! We waited on His will and kept faith with Him right to the end. You have no right to accuse us of abandoning you! Go away! We don't want to talk to you any more!"

"You will see, wicked woman. You will see! God will punish you for denying us Christian charity in our hour of need." At that, Ron stormed out to his car and screeched off down the road.

When Jack came home, he found me in tears. "I can't stand this any more, I just want to go home," I sobbed brokenly. "I want to go back to California." To my surprise and relief, he agreed.

"I think that's a great idea. Let's go right away. I want to leave, too. I've had enough of this."

Within two days, we were packed and on the road home. Back in California, with God's grace, Jack landed a teaching job in the public school in Hillsdale, my hometown.

We were free, or so I thought.

Jack and I somehow put our lives back together. We reestablished ties with our families and bought a house. We were enjoying a somewhat normal life, though I still insisted we look more to our spiritual needs, and we were not as outgoing with others as we had been before. We bought a little pop-up camper trailer, and in the summers we'd go camping with our kids in the mountains. Jack was studying for his master's degree, which would allow him to progress and earn more money. Although we still hadn't achieved the spiritual perfection I longed for, our life became relatively peaceful and happy.

Despite this, I thought about the Larrinagas a lot and worried about them, but I felt God must be taking care of them. After a few months, probably in a feeling of Christian fellowship, Jack wrote to Ron and told him where he worked.

Now and then after that, Jack would get a postcard from Ron, always sent to him at work. I never heard anything from Ron myself. I was sure it was his way of punishing me for my "rebelliousness." Sometimes, curiously, I missed them, missed him. Then I would push them from my mind, like a bad dream.

Then one day Jack got a call at the school where he worked, from Ron Larrinaga. "We need your help," Ron said, "and we beg you for some Christian charity. We'll be coming through California soon, and we need a place to stay for a few days before we go on with our trip. We're heading for Oregon and then Colorado, where I'll be doing missionary work. We are in need. 'Therefore to him that knoweth to do good, and doeth it not, to him it is sin.'" Jack didn't know what to do. Ron's last quotation had gotten him, as Ron knew it would.

"Well, I guess it would be okay for a couple of days, Ron, but I have to check with Mary. She was very upset with you when we left Arizona, you know. I'll check with her tonight and see what she says. Call me again tomorrow, okay?"

But Ron didn't call back. They just appeared at our door with all their kids and a big German shepherd dog in tow. Strangely, June was not with them, though I was too overwhelmed by the confusion of all the people to notice that at first. When they all piled in, Jack and I looked at each other in despair, and then he shrugged. What could we do? I was shaken at the thought of all those people and that big dog messing up my nice little house. Then I was ashamed of my lack of Christian charity. "Well, I guess we can stand it for just a few days," I told him as we settled down for the night.

"I can't deny them Christian charity if they are in need, and I'm really pleased to see the children again. They look like they need a good meal, as always."

Within two days, Ron took over our house. He dictated our lives as he had before, as though it was his place and not ours. When we asked them why they were in California and not in Arizona any more, Ron said he had been obliged to get a part-time job to keep them going. His dispute with the school officials had continued. "June was impossible about consorting with the heathen," Ron said. "She had to be punished constantly."

"Where is June?" I asked. They were both evasive at first, but I persisted.

Finally, Ron said, "We had to leave her behind."

"Leave her behind?" I said, shocked. "With whom? What do you mean?"

Janet shrugged and didn't look directly at me. "I really don't know. One day, Johnny came home crying, without June. He told his father the teachers had kept June and wouldn't let her come home with him."

"Kept her? How could they just keep her? They can't do that, can they?

Ron took up the story. "Well, they did. A detective came to the house and interrogated me. He had the nerve to accuse me of neglect and abuse of June! He asked a lot of questions about June, and about us and about our life at home. I told him we were a good Christian family, just trying to live our life according to God's will. When he left, I could see he wasn't satisfied with what I'd told him."

"So then what happened?" I pressed.

"Why, God warned me to leave there immediately," he

said. "I knew God's will was primary, so we packed up and left Arizona that very night, and here we are," he finished.

I was stunned. "You left, just like that? Without June? Without your own daughter? How could you do that? She's only a child! What will happen to her now?" Janet had begun sobbing softly. Ron gave her a sharp poke with his elbow and an angry glare, and she became quiet. He himself showed no emotion about abandoning his child to strangers. "How could you have left without her?" I demanded.

"It was God's will," he said complacently, as though that explained all, and the subject was closed.

Jack was as shocked as I was. We'd had our fourth child that year. I couldn't imagine leaving him or any of our children anywhere, especially not knowing what happened to them. It made me shiver to think of it.

However, June's predicament soon faded from our consciousness in the turmoil of so many people staying in our little house, not to mention their huge, hungry, noisy dog. "I wish they'd keep him penned up outside somehow," I said to Jack. But when he tried, the dog barked incessantly, annoying the neighbors. They were already annoyed at all the kids running up and down the neighborhood.

After a week of having them in residence, Jack and I were getting nervous. The Larrinagas showed no signs of starting out on their missionary trip. "Where is it you're heading? Oregon?" Jack prompted Ron hopefully that night after dinner.

"Yes, eventually we want to go there and do mission-ary work among the heathen," Ron answered.

"When do you plan to start out?"

"Oh, soon, probably," he replied vaguely. "God will

tell me when it's His will for us to go." God must have been occupied with other matters just then, because they didn't leave. They stayed on and on. They behaved as though our home belonged to them.

Ron preached at me constantly, ordering me and the children around. After having lived alone without them, I resented the work it took for us to feed them all and clean up after them. The house had been reduced to a shambles by the kids and the dog. Finally, Jack took the reins and ordered them to leave. "Sorry, folks, but you have to go. We can't keep on supporting you like this, and you're intruding on our lives and our household. You'll have to leave and go on with your trip."

Ron refused to budge. "We are not going until God wills it for us. He will send me a sign. You are being very un-Christian," he accused, glaring at me, "and disobedient to the will of God for you! You are turning us out into the wilderness with no place to rest our heads. God will bring down his wrath upon your head for disobedience to His word." Feeling guilty, we backed off. A few more days passed. Again, Jack tried to get them to leave, but they just wouldn't go. Jack and Ron fought. Jack and I fought.

Ron worked on both of us. "Your unhappiness is a result of your continual consorting with the heathen. You have lost your true direction and your faith in God's will for you. Look at you, concerned only with things of the flesh, with this house, with your possessions! It is your spiritual life that is in starvation and you cannot even see that! You have abandoned God's word, and His teachings! You have become wicked, wicked people! Now I know why God sent me here to you, to save you from the error of your foolish ways! It was His will that I leave Arizona and come here for He saw to what depths you had sunk. He sent me, the chosen servant of Jesus Christ, to save you from the abyss."

At his words, I was again filled with guilt and confusion. My old longing, perhaps obsession, for religion returned. We had been lax in our spiritual life, I conceded, and maybe we were allowing too much of the godless spirit to creep into our lives, but, on the other hand, having been away from his influence for a while, I wasn't so sure that Ron's way was the right way. I waffled and wavered. He didn't let up on me, or on Jack. He harangued us endlessly, especially Jack. "You are wasting your talent teaching in the heathen schools! You consort with the godless daily. No wonder you have forsaken God's will and His word!"

Before long, I was under his influence again. Jack stopped demanding that they leave. I accepted Ron's constant demands on me and spent my days shopping for food, cooking, and cleaning for the whole mob. June was never mentioned, nor was their trip to Oregon. Ron continued to run my household as though it was his own. I gave control completely over to him. Jack went to work, came home, ate, and listened to Ron's sermons at night. Alone in our room, we fell into exhausted sleep. We did not discuss our new situation. We just accepted it.

One Sunday, my parents came to visit us. They were furious to discover that the Larrinagas were there, firmly encamped in our home. They didn't bother with politeness. My father didn't care who heard him. "Are you crazy?" he yelled at me. "What are you doing, letting all these people stay in your house for weeks on end? Feeding them, giving them everything Jack earns! Throw them out! They're bums!

Tell them to get out and get their own place. These people are nuts, Mary. They're blood suckers! You have to get rid of them!"

Unfortunately, pride threw me firmly to the Larrinaga's side. I felt a need to defend what we were doing to my parents. I tried to soothe my father and explain to him about charity, about sharing God's bounty, and about my spiritual needs and my Christian conscience. "Please don't get so upset, Dad. The Larrinagas are in need just now, and it's our Christian duty to help them, according to the will of God."

"Will of God, my ass!" stormed my father, who was having none of it. "Let him get a job and see what the will of God is to work for a living like the rest of us! And you," he looked at me in a strange way, "need to get off this kick, Mary. I don't know, but there's something wrong with you and Jack now. You haven't been yourselves since you went to Arizona. And this isn't right, to live like this, to deprive your own children for the sake of these . . . these . . ." He sputtered, looking for a word. "Damned leeches!"

"Please, Brian," my mother said, trying to calm him down. She was upset because we were fighting, and I was crying. And no wonder I was crying: my nerves were in shambles. My mother tried to make peace. "I'm sure they'll be gone soon. Mary and Jack must know what they're doing. Maybe we should go now and come back again next week when they're gone?" she said hopefully.

But my father would not be mollified. "Go? Why should WE go?" he shouted. "We're Mary's family, and they're not! You think they'll go as long as there's a free meal around? And a free roof over their heads? They'll never

64

leave! Not while they've got their hooks into our kids! They're the worst kind of leeches. Jack is supporting them all, for Chrissake! Look what a mess they made of their lives the last time this weasel showed up!"

He turned to me, and there was no mistaking the look in his eyes. "Well, I wash my hands of this whole thing! You do what you want, Mary. But don't say I didn't warn you. Your mother and I don't approve of this, and we certainly don't approve of what you're doing with your kids and your life. This nonsense has gone too far!" With that, my father stormed out the door.

My mother hugged me to her. "Take care, child. You're a good girl, but this man has you all mixed up. You need to think for yourself. Don't let these people take over your life." She kissed me gently on the cheek. Then she followed Dad out. Sadly, wishing that they understood, I watched them go. I didn't realize that would be the last time I'd ever see my mother.

Ron stepped in immediately. "You see now," he said, "how your parents are hopeless heathen, how they are yet unsaved? They claim to be Christian, but they are un-Christian, uncharitable! They are under the influence of Satan and are trying to influence you to follow them in the ways of Satan, away from God's will for you! You must not let them do this to you, Mary. If they cannot and will not see God's will for them, how can they see His will for you? If you listen to them you will be cast out from God's grace as Adam and Eve were! You will be condemned to following Satan and his ways."

I was disturbed and confused. In the weeks that followed, I called my parents several times and tried to get them to understand my spiritual position. They didn't budge. "You know, you need to look to your own salvation, too," I told my mother. "You should be less concerned with money and temporal things and more concerned with God's will for you in life." Ron had been bugging me to work to convert my parents to our way of thinking, to come with us and follow him as the chosen servant of Jesus Christ, and to commit their lives completely to God. They refused to listen to my entreaties. My father wouldn't even come to the phone.

"Your father is deeply hurt, and so am I," said my mother. "You're allowing this man to cut you off from us, and we don't like how he dominates you, and you let him. You kowtow to his every whim, and it's not good. You need to get rid of him, all of them, now. I know it's hard seeing all those children so deprived, but you have children, too, Mary, and you must think of them and of Jack. He can't keep supporting that whole crowd."

This went on for weeks. Finally, in desperation, my parents sent my oldest brother, Kevin, to the house to try to talk to us, to intervene. Ron didn't let me answer the door. "You cannot speak with him, you must cast him out. He is a heathen, he has been sent by Satan to turn you away from what is God's will for you!" At that point, I believed Ron. I believed what he said, that Kevin was an agent of Satan, sent to turn us away from God's will for us. "To show your obedience to God, you must deny your brother, turn him away." I did as ordered. I turned my own brother away from my door. It had taken Ron just over a month to get me under his thumb and his spell, again.

"That is good. You did right, and God will be pleased. You must not allow your family to interfere with what God is doing in your life!" Ron said. That was a rare pat on the back for me. I felt inordinately proud that finally I had done something that pleased him, that pleased God, in the eyes of his chosen servant, Ron. It gave me confidence that I was finding the right spiritual path, at last. Jack, too, had fallen back into Ron's web during that month. At his command, we excluded our families from our lives and stopped calling them. After awhile, they stopped trying to see us. Once again, Ron triumphed.

I failed to see the danger. I didn't see that, with every victory over our wills, with every move we conceded to him, with every desire to please him, with the alienation of our families and our associates, Ron Larrinaga gained more of his objective. As my father predicted, the Larrinagas didn't leave. Nor did we ask them to go.

Eight months later, Ron again demanded that Jack quit his job. "We'll go to Florida," he said. "All of us, together."

"I don't know, Ron," said Jack. "I have a good job here, and we like our house."

"Jack, you must leave the public schools once and for all and teach in a good Christian school where you can get away from teaching the heathen and interacting with them every day. I can get you a position at a Christian school in Florida. I know the principal there, and we can stay with another family, the Millers, who want to join us." Ron was very confident, very persuasive.

"Okay, we'll try it, but not until after the end of the school year," Jack said. For once, Ron didn't dispute him.

That summer we put our house up for sale, and it sold quickly. Ron was so anxious to leave that we didn't even wait to complete the sale or to notify our families of what we were doing. Instead, we left for Florida, and, at Ron's instruction, Jack sent a registered letter to my father, asking him to go to Hillsdale and complete the sale, since any proceeds that would come from it were rightfully his. My parents had loaned us the money to buy the house.

Jack gave Dad the Millers' address in Florida. When we arrived, there was a registered letter there from Dad. He didn't mince words. "The sale of the house fell through. HAVE YOU COMPLETELY TAKEN LEAVE OF YOUR SENSES?" That last was in big letters, obviously written in fury. "Now what do you expect me do do?" My heart fell. Now we'd still have the mortgage to pay.

"Ignore him," Ron ordered me. "Do not reply. He will handle things as best he can. God will help him, for He knows we are here to do His will." I was upset about dumping everything on my father like that, but Ron was adamant. My insides churned constantly during the next months. However, I saw Ron as a profound, righteous man of God, intent on pleasing the Almighty rather than pleasing people. My father just didn't understand Ron, I thought, the way we did. How could he? My father hadn't dedicated his life totally to Christ and to following the word of God, without compromise, the way Ron had.

We moved in, all of us, with Katherine and Sam Miller and their daughter Kathleen who was almost eighteen. I'm sure they were astonished and shocked at so many house guests—more than a dozen—but they accepted us with good spirit. Soon, Ron began working on them, trying to bring them under his influence. He harangued them at great length, quoting reams of Scripture. He told them they were not following God's word and God's will for their lives. Before

long, he had them looking bewildered and confused. He kept
increasing religious pressure on them, and I noticed that he
was browbeating poor Katherine and their daughter in much
the same way he did me. Katherine ran around cooking and
cleaning for all of us, and Ron did nothing but hold forth
every day on God's spiritual will for their lives and act like
he owned the place. They were too upset and confused by it
all to challenge him, or us.

To my surprise, Ron and Jack suddenly started bicker-
ing, like two kids, over every little thing. They'd come to see
me to referee. If I didn't side with Ron, he'd turn on me. If I
did, Jack would get angry at me. I had become Ron's target,
his ultimate prey, and to get me, he had to first alienate me
from my husband.

One day, I said or did something that infuriated Ron.
He turned on me and slapped me hard across the face. The
blow sent me reeling. Jack didn't come to my assistance.
"You are rebellious," Ron shouted, "and your husband is too
much of a coward to teach you to submit! He should teach
you to bend to God's will and not let you be such an evil,
unsubmissive woman! Go to your room! You'll stay there
and think about your sins until I decide you can come out
again." I turned and ran for the security of my room. Ron
made me stay there, with only rice and water to eat, for three
days. Deep inside, I sensed that things had taken a wrong
turn, that my life was suddenly spinning out of control, but I
was too proud to face what was happening. I refused to run
away, or go crawling back to my family. I thought a lot during those three days. This had to do with my spiritual state,
after all. What I wanted for my life was to serve Christ. I
wanted to follow His dictates. As Ron had said, I was being

punished for being rebellious. He had chastised me for my rebellion, for my refusal to bend my will to God's. And I *was* rebellious, I reasoned. I resented leaving California, and I resented having to sell our house. Ron was right. I was not "willing to be willing." I had not properly submitted my will to God's. In my room, I mentally reviewed all my human failings and finally came to the conclusion that I had deserved Ron hitting me. I deserved Jack's disdain.

Humbly, I asked God for forgiveness and resolved to do better, to try to please God, and vowed to submit my will to what God wanted of me, through Ron, His chosen servant. It was a long time after that before Ron hit me gain, which reinforced my belief that I had deserved it.

The Millers, meanwhile, were also under his spell. Ron had them convinced that they, too, were in a poor spiritual state. "You are rebellious and not properly submitting to the will of God in providing for us and our Christian needs!" he scolded Mrs. Miller. "You are compromising God's doctrine and His will for you," he chided Sam Miller.

With our cramped quarters and meager earnings, Ron and Jack were soon arguing in earnest. Jack's job had fallen through, and the lease on the Millers' house was running out. Finally, Jack could stand it no longer. "I'm through with you and your long-winded sermons," he told Ron. "I'm glad that we have to leave this house. When we leave, you just go your way and we'll go ours. We're going back to California, and without you! I don't want any more of this togetherness. You are not welcome in our home." Ron started in again with a stream of invective and accusations that we were un-Christian and abandoning his children to starvation and poverty. "Here, you can take this with you, and I don't care where you go." Jack gave him the keys to our pop-up camper trailer, so the kids wouldn't have to sleep out in the open, or in the car.

I didn't care what they did, either. At that point, as in Arizona, I never wanted to see the Larrinagas again. We headed back to California, hoping our house was still empty and available. Then, as we crossed the Tombigbee River in Alabama, we came upon a terrible accident in which several young children had been killed and several others badly injured. We stopped to assist them. Afterwards, shaken, I was convinced God was showing us his anger for sending the Larrinagas away, for leaving those children without shelter or a home. I said to Jack, "We could have been in that accident. God spared us our lives and our children to humble us by seeing what He could have done to us, so we would learn and repent our selfish, rebellious ways." That night, I fell on my knees in the little motel and thanked God for giving us another chance. I promised Him I would help the Larrinagas if they needed it in the future. "I will follow your will for me and act with Christian charity as You have commanded," I vowed.

When we got back to California after four hard days of driving, we found our house empty. Although our life returned to normal again on the outside, behind closed doors things were profoundly different. Our lives had been forever changed by Ron Larrinaga's influence. We stayed pretty much to ourselves, avoiding our families except for an occasional visit or phone call, and we had absolutely no social life. We didn't rejoin our old church, and we avoided contact with the community. We were loners now, clinging to the separatist life that Ron had instilled in us, worshipping God in our own way, without external perspective to guide us. Jack did not hesitate to demand "obedience and submission" from me. Our fifth child, Jimmy, was born a year later.

We had an occasional letter from the Larrinagas after we left. They seemed to be traveling around. The letters came from Virginia, Texas, New York, the Carolinas, and then Florida again, near Hobe Sound. Then one day I was out shopping, and I found a bin of socks on sale for ten dollars for the whole bin. It had every imaginable color and size of socks in it. "Those would be great for the Larrinaga kids," I thought to myself. I remembered that they were wearing socks with holes in them the last time I saw them. Impulsively, I bought the whole bin. "I'll mail it to them next week. Janet will be glad to get this," I murmured. But I didn't need to mail them. When I got home that day, I found the Larrinagas and Millers, along with their daughter, standing on my patio. They were broke, worn out, and "seeking Christian refuge." I sighed in despair. But remembering my vow to God that day in Alabama, I opened the door and took them in.

Before an hour had passed, Ron had my stomach in knots and me feeling guilty and unworthy. I remembered the accident—all those dead and injured kids!—and swallowed my resentment. I would show Christian charity. Janet had given birth to three more children, Hannah, Sheila, and Charles. June was never mentioned. One night, I asked if they'd heard any more from her, or about her. Janet just turned away, and Ron berated me for mentioning her name. "Do not speak of her, wicked girl! She is gone, as God willed it! From babyhood, that girl had a resistance to God and to obedience," he declared vehemently. "I had a dream that she was in a pit, a deep, dark pit, and she was trying to grab my hand as I leaned over to help her. I thought I could pull her out of the pit, but, in reality, she was trying to pull me down into the pit with her! God showed me in my dream that this was the terrible spiritual condition of the girl, that she was trying to destroy the will of God in my life! Her rebellious behavior brought a reproach upon the name of Christ. God told me I must leave her and save myself. Do not mention that godless child in this house!" I shut up and never mentioned her again.

Occasionally, the Larrinagas and Millers left us, to go on the road so Ron could do missionary work, he said. "We are trying to convert others to accept the will of God for them, like you."

To preserve some shred of peace and sanity in our household, Jack and I put the money down to buy the Larrinagas a new tent trailer. I couldn't stand to think of all those children sleeping in that pitiful, worn out pop-up trailer we had given them back in Florida. It was torn in places and leaked badly, and it had no toilet facilities. Yet they, the Millers, and their children had actually been living in it most of the time since they'd left us, Janet told me. I could see in her expression how awful it had been for her. "We have to do something to help them and get them out of here for at least a few weeks at a time," I said.

So we got them not only the bigger tent trailer, but a used station wagon to pull it. With those, they traveled here and there, returning to us for a month or two at a time between trips. At one point they lived for a while with a couple in Pennsylvania Ron was sure he had converted. His next target was a military family in Colorado, Everett and Sally

Spencer and their son Johnny, who was in his early twenties. Ron, taking Janet along, made quite a few trips there and spent a lot of time with them. I felt guilty when I prayed that they would move in with the Spencers. However, the Larrinagas were involved in an accident in Nevada, and the station wagon and trailer were destroyed. Ron called to give us the bad news. "Luckily, we were all spared, by the will and grace of God," he said.

Jack was fit to be tied when they returned to California and casually moved in with us again. "In Arizona, I said I never wanted to see them again, and I said it again in Florida, and yet they keep showing up on our doorstep!" he complained. "We can't keep on like this, Mary. I don't care what you promised God you'd do. Christian charity or not, they're breaking us. That tent and station wagon cost us a bundle! He never works to pay for anything, so what does he care?"

"Shhh, they'll hear you," I soothed. "It will be all right, you'll see. God will provide. God will reward you for your goodness."

By then we had sold our house in Hillsdale and rented a house in Calmont, closer to where Jack worked. I talked Jack into buying us a new Pace Arrow motor home. "We can let the Larrinagas use it for their missionary trips, and we'll use it ourselves, in the summers, to take our own family and go on vacations to the mountains. That way we'll get away from them more." Jack grudgingly went along with the idea, but even with the Pace Arrow at their command, the Larrinagas did not seem interested in traveling as much as before.

"I need to be here to look after your Christian souls and those of the others. I need to teach you the way to please

God. You seem to be falling back into your old heathen ways," he said forcefully.

From that day on, his control over us was suddenly more direct, more forceful, and, very soon, more physically brutal. In fact, it was overpowering. He started disciplining our children, hitting them, then beating them with a belt, whenever they disobeyed or violated a rule. "I am doing this because you won't," he told us, "and children need discipline according to God's word." He would then quote from the Old Testament about how it was good to beat your children. All the children were routinely hit with belts, wooden spoons, or hairbrushes.

Then he told us Jack or I were to interrogate our children as soon as they came home from school every day. "It is your responsibility as God-fearing Christian parents to assure that they have no social interaction there with the unsaved." That task usually fell to me, or to Kathleen Miller, who was his lieutenant and disciplinarian, since Jack was still at work when they came home from school. If they did anything at school that Ron didn't agree with, they were immediately punished. Any infraction by any of the children merited their pants being stripped off, and they got a severe whipping with a belt. "What you've done is against the will of God for you," he'd tell them, as they screamed and cried in pain. "You must never do it again."

If they lied, or tried to hide things from us, we'd say, "Don't try to lie and hide things from us. We'll find out, and then you'll be doubly punished, doubly whipped. Now try to do better tomorrow." The whippings were almost a daily occurrence, and Philip, Marian, Louise, and David, who had until now been such cheerful, happy kids, soon became fearful and withdrawn. They cried, and they lied. I went along meekly with whatever Ron ordered done to them. I was afraid of him, and he knew it and exploited it.

Jack responded by withdrawing from us all. He'd study the Bible with Ron, and they'd argue philosophy and God's word, but seemed to be resigned to whatever happened. It's your game, he seemed to be saying to me, though he never said that in so many words. You want them here, you handle it. Anxious to finally test my ability to please Ron, and, through him, to please God, I gave myself and all of us completely over to Ron's control. He grasped the reins of total authority with vigor and imposed his cruel domination on me and the children with a vengeance. However, the children and I, as well as the others, were punished mostly when Jack wasn't around.

By then Ron was ordering me to beat my children. I'd try to be easier on them than he was. I'd make a lot of noise like I was hitting them much harder than I was. But Ron soon saw through that. The next time he felt Marian needed to be whipped, he sent Kathleen in with the belt to beat her. I objected. "You question my orders?" he shouted and grabbed me by the arm. "I'll show you what disobedience gets you! Kathleen! Come here and help me administer some discipline to this wicked woman."

He and Kathleen dragged me to my room and threw me across the bed. She threw up my skirt and pulled down my panties, and then she beat me with a belt until I cried for mercy, while he watched. "Yes, say you're sorry!" he said. "You have offended the will of God with your rebelliousness!"

"I'm sorry!" I screamed. The pain was agonizing, and

76

Kathleen wasn't stopping. I couldn't believe I was being hit, let alone by one of the children. I twisted and turned, trying to get away, but Kathleen wasn't a child any more. She was over twenty, and Ron had trained her to be "the family" disciplinarian. Kathleen swung that belt down on my bare buttocks with ferocity, as I screamed and cried. Ron always made sure the radio was on, playing loudly, to cover my cries. Finally, sobbing and begging God and Ron to forgive me, I admitted being rebellious.

"There, that's enough," he said finally, and Kathleen stopped. I clutched my skirt around me to cover my nakedness and rolled over on the bed, just wanting to die there. Ron slammed the door and went out, leaving me alone. "Think about your sins against God!" he commanded as he left.

Soon the landlord began complaining about having so many people living in the house and about all the kids and the noise. "The other neighbors are calling and complaining," he said. Ron quickly packed up his extended family and took off for a few weeks in the motor home, not wanting to alert the authorities to how many kids were living in that house and not going to school, or the other things going on there.

By then, on Ron's orders, I had taken Louise and Marian out of school. "Marian is behaving strangely lately. I think she is being fooled around with at that heathen school, by one of the boys in her class," Ron said. I never suspected what was probably the real truth, that it was Ron himself who was "fooling around" with Marian, not one of the boys in her class. He was just using that as a cover.

Once, he ordered Marian whipped, and Kathleen beat

her so hard across her bare buttocks and thighs with a belt that angry red welts sprang up, and Marian screamed and shrieked, trying to get away, crying and begging her to stop, but it just went on and on. Finally, I couldn't stand it. I ran in and pulled Kathleen away from Marian, screaming, "Stop! You're killing her! Stop!" I tried to grab the belt, which had been cut in strips like a cat-o-nine tail, out of her hand. But Kathleen was stronger than I was. She twisted my arm and threw me across the bed and began beating me with it. Marian crawled to a corner and cowered there, shaking and crying in terror. Ron was sitting at the kitchen table, and he paid no heed to our screams and cries.

Kathleen kept lashing away, harder and harder. She grunted with effort as she swung the belt over and over. I thought I was going to die if she didn't stop. In desperation, I gathered strength and broke away from her, rolling off the bed. I scrambled toward the door, but she came after me, lashing me about the head and shoulders and yelling, "Will you submit now? Do you repent your rebelliousness before God?"

"Yes! I'm sorry," I cried. "Stop, please stop, I repent!" It seemed forever before she stopped and left me lying there on the floor, sobbing and whimpering in pain. It was the most brutal beating yet, but it was nothing compared to what was to come later, for all of us.

Ron would take some of the extended family, and, occasionally, one or two of my children, on his missionary trips and leave one or two of his lieutenants, usually Kathleen Miller and Johnny Spencer, behind to be sure we stayed in line while they were gone. That summer, Ron and Janet were in Colorado on a missionary trip where they had their twelfth child, Luke. When they returned in September and moved back in with us, our landlord promptly served us with an eviction notice. It was then that Ron first pressed me into writing letters to people in authority and taught me to deny, to protest, and to fight back whenever authorities tried to intrude on our lives.

In this instance, it was to no avail. In June, we were ordered by a judge to vacate our house. I cried in despair. I didn't know what would happen to us now. Ron beat me severely, for not being able to convince the judge. Then I was ordered to stand at the end of the hall, facing the wall, hands clasped behind my back, for hours, and to sleep there on the cold floor at night. A few days later, when we had to move out, Ron took Janet, the others, and his kids and took off in the motor home, ordering me to find another place for us all to live.

"God will provide," Ron assured me. I watched him drive away with his family. He had our motor home, the one we were making payments on. Jack and I and our children were homeless.

But by then I feared Ron more than I detested him, and I obeyed him unquestioningly. I knew well what the consequences would be if I didn't. Jack took refuge in apathy, and Ron left Jack pretty much alone, as long as Jack turned over his paycheck to him. Jack continued to study his Bible in the evenings with Ron, but, aside from that, he paid little attention to what went on in our home.

On Ron's missionary trips, it was Johnny who was Ron's workhorse. Ron taught him to steal and to siphon gas out of other cars, particularly out of county vehicles parked along the side of the road where work crews were doing road

work. Johnny was over six-foot tall and worked out with
weights. He was also trained by Ron to be the surveillance
and intelligence operative for the extended family. He was
allowed to overlook nothing and had to report every action,
every gesture, every facial expression, every word spoken,
back to Ron, who would then open his Bible and look into it,
like some sort of seer, and interpret the meaning of what
Johnny had told him according to where the Bible was opened
"by the hand of God." When he'd return, Ron would continue
working to alienate Jack and me. I didn't object though he kept
us separated and without money, so we couldn't "corrupt"
each other, or escape from him.

By the time we were evicted from the house in
Calmont, our savings were gone. Ron had bled us dry. He
never worked. He was too busy interpreting the word of God
and keeping us all in line. We were frugal, made all our own
clothes, used electricity sparingly, ate little, but still Jack's
meager salary wouldn't stretch to support so many.

To save on food bills, we retrieved discarded food out
of the garbage bins behind the supermarkets in town. It was
usually my job to take one or two of the boys and drive
around in the afternoons and pick through them for usable
food. I hated going on those garbage runs. I hated picking
through trash. I was fastidious and neat and had never had to
resort to living like this. "Waste not, want not," Ron would
intone. "God provides in His way."

So we'd go out and do it, and it was surprising how
much edible food we got that way. I called it "garbaging,"
but little Jimmy couldn't pronounce that and came up with
"bygering." "We're going out bygering," he'd say, and that

became the family word for what we did those afternoons, so no one else would know we were garbage picking.

"Who went bygering today?" Ron would ask every night. We got not only food, but hundreds of slightly wilted flowering plants and herbs for our garden, plucked from the trash bins of nurseries and florists. I loved bringing them back to life and seeing them perk up and bloom again.

Ron also taught some of the older boys to switch prices on merchandise at the stores, then talk to distract the cashiers when checking out, so the clerks wouldn't notice what they'd done. When I objected to him "teaching the children to be *thieves*," he had me whipped again by Kathleen.

"It is not thievery!" he snarled at me. "It is only fair repayment to us for bringing the word of God to the ungrateful heathen." Ron often beat the others himself, but he always had someone else beat me on my bare bottom, while he stood and watched.

One day, when Ron was whipping Katherine Miller for not "wiping that look off your face," and she was crying and begging him to stop, I found myself wondering why God wanted all this pain and suffering from us? Hadn't we honestly tried to submit our lives and hearts to him? What was it we had overlooked that we still must suffer so? What hadn't we done? We had sacrificed and humiliated ourselves, we had offered Christian charity to the Larrinagas and taken them in. We had given up our families and all our worldly possessions to try to please God. What more could there be?

I didn't know how much more, because I had no idea how crazy Ron Larrinaga really was. By then, we had all become his mindlessly obedient pawns, his acolytes, his loyal lieutenants. Completely out of touch with reality, we were convinced that Ron was, as he continually insisted, "the chosen servant of Jesus Christ, sent by God to lead you out of sin. Only by submitting yourselves to my will can you hope to be saved." So we submitted, and submitted, and submitted, so that we could be saved. Our move to the hills of Tartola, California, brought us all to the depths of an unimaginable torture that was everyday life with Ron Larrinaga. That any of us lived through it was a miracle, that we continued following him brought us to the entrance to hell.

4

terror in tartola

My wounds, and those of my children, turned blue, and many times the blows to my face were so heavy that I fainted. Black eyes were worn like a mask, and my cheeks burned fiery red from slaps that sent me reeling. "Don't you dare fall down!" Ron would shout. "Get up, wicked woman, get up or I'll drag you up!" He'd grab me by my long hair and drag me across the floor and around the room by it.

"Oh God, oh God, what have I done?" I'd cry out. "Why must I suffer so?"

I could no longer reason, no longer find a cause, let alone a cure for the prison I was in. Ron Larrinaga, after sinking his evil fangs into us back in San Luis Obispo had become our obsession, and the venom in his heart had slowly and insistently infected us until our minds and bodies were paralyzed, unable to think or reason competently. I continued to go along with Ron as a docile follower, beyond ability to escape the hell in which I had become trapped.

Ron needed to control us completely, in mind and body, in soul and spirit. He needed to enslave us in order to bend us to his depraved will.

That summer we found a four-bedroom house for sale high up in the hills in Tartola. Almost no money down was required. Somehow Jack and I managed to qualify for a mortgage to buy it. By then there were nearly thirty adults and children living together. The house was almost hidden in the big trees and tangled brush around it. There was a six-foot high cedar board fence separating us from our neighbors, which Ron liked because he was sure the neighbors—the "unsaved heathen" as he called them—watched and spied on us all the time. He always went to great lengths to document and photograph anyone he felt was spying on him, or us. He had become so paranoid that he ordered us to keep the drapes drawn day and night, and the children hidden from sight.

The basis for daily life with Ron Larrinaga thereafter was a quotation from the Book of Matthew that he would resort to over and over again as he played us one against the other, controlled our every move, and punished us unmercifully.

> Think not that I am come to send peace on earth:
> I came not to send peace, but a sword.
> For I am come
> To set a man at variance against his father
> And the daughter against her mother . . .
> A man's foes shall be they of his own household.

Matthew 10:34-36

The isolation and high fencing allowed Ron to exercise rigid control over us, to whip and torment us, with less fear of interruption or interference. Even so, there were drawbacks from Ron's point of view. We were on a hillside, and a road wound around above the house in the back, and along that road were a number of occupied homes. The people in those homes could see down into our yard, and that worried Ron. He didn't want anyone to be able to see us.

He was especially pleased with the intercom system that came with the house. It had speakers to all the rooms and at the front and back doors. That allowed us to answer the doors without opening them and meant that no one would ever be able to take him by surprise. He could also play loud music over the system, which would cover the sounds of the beatings and abuse day and night. And the outside speakers meant he could blare his music and endless religious tirades up at the neighbors. He loved that and was soon doing it.

The house was a split plan. The Larrinagas and the others were at one end, with three smaller bedrooms, family room, and bath, while Jack and I were for the time being given the other end of the house, with the master bedroom and bath. The living room and kitchen, situated in between, were shared by everyone. We didn't realize it at first but the divided floor plan would also make it easy for Ron to isolate anyone he wanted to, which increased his ability to punish and control all of us.

Total isolation after severe physical punishment was one of his favorite methods. He'd banish anyone he wanted punished to one end of the house for weeks, or months. He wouldn't let them speak to or associate with anyone else. They stayed alone, while everyone else stayed in the other end.

The little children were concealed inside the house most of the time. Once in a while, but not often, he'd allow them to play outside on the back patio. But later, as the neighbors became suspicious of us and began interfering, even that short play period outdoors was ruled out. It was at that time that Ron produced some guns. "To protect us," he said.

One warm July afternoon, I stood in the corner of our bedroom, with a pair of my underpants soaked with my own urine draped over my head, the wet crotch drawn squarely over my nose. Exhausted, wretched, burning with pain from a whipping, I dared not even cry out, or whimper. My tears of humiliation mixed with the urine sliding down my cheeks, and the ammonia fumes burned my eyes. I almost choked, unable to breathe. I had been beaten until I could barely stand, beaten until I wet myself in pain and terror. Blood was everywhere in the room, spattered on the walls, the bed, and drying in a dark stain on the belt with which Kathleen had just finished whipping me.

Suddenly the door opened. Ron stepped into the room and stood there glaring, waiting for all the children to file in behind him. I stood with my hands clasped behind my back, and, when I heard his step, my knees began shaking again with terror. There was silence until the children had all assembled. Then, Ron raised his arm dramatically and pointed at me. "Look at her!" he commanded loudly. "Look at that wicked woman! Shame on her, wetting her pants! She's an adult! This just shows how foolish and irresponsible she is, and why I have to whip her to make her realize her role and responsibility in this home! How can she ever obey God and understand spiritual matters when she can't even control her own body? How can I teach her the deep realities of God when she has no mind except to lie around and be useless?" By then his voice had risen to a shout.

I couldn't see their faces clearly, but I knew the children were all standing there round-eyed, staring solemnly at me, nodding their heads yes, as Ron pointed out my "faults" to one and all. Then they turned and parroted his accusations to each other, as they had been taught to do. "Yes, wicked woman!" they said.

"She has wet herself."

"She must be punished."

"She must repent her sins!"

"She must learn to obey."

"She must follow God's will for her."

None of the children went to school any more. Our youngest, Ellen, was only two. Jimmy, our seven-year-old, had never gone to school, and I had removed Marian and David from their classes in elementary school and junior high. Louise was removed at ninth grade level. Only Philip, our oldest, went as far as his junior year in high school.

Now I stood there in abject humiliation and heard my own children ridicule me. "Yes! Look at her!" one child, it sounded like Jimmy, said loudly.

"Look at the wicked woman! She can't even control her own body!"

"Yes, look at her," said another. "She has wet her pants, and now she has to wear them on her head. She must be punished for her transgressions."

Ron launched into another of his long diatribes, railing against me, hurling insults and accusations at me, calling me a "harlot who has disgraced herself before God!" The children stood and listened as Ron had trained them to do. Burning with pain and shame, weak from hunger, I felt helpless and terrified. "Do not speak!" Ron commanded me, though I was too frightened to even think of making a sound, "and do not move! You will stand still and listen and learn about your wicked ways."

Sometimes he ranted on for an hour or more before he stopped and went out. More often than not, he'd have a drink in his hand when giving his harangue. He had begun drinking heavily and was more brutal than ever when he'd had a few drinks. But finally he'd get tired and stop, or realize that his drink was empty, and he'd leave. Now, he finished. The children followed him out, and I was left standing, facing the corner, hands behind my back. I knew I'd stand there like that for twelve hours, or fourteen or more, not daring to move or change position, the wet panties slowly drying on my head.

This horrible treatment of physical beatings followed by public humiliation had been going on for years in the Larrinaga home, but had only recently been introduced into our lives. We were, as I call it now, put into the "pit" of beatings, terror, manipulation, harangue, and humiliation. The children were always stripped naked when they were beaten, and then the others were called in to look at their bruises and mock them. Standing beaten and humiliated while the others pointed and mocked was the ultimate degradation, the real soul-breaker. I remembered how, back in Arizona, Ron had taken all his children in to look at and taunt poor little June, standing naked and shivering in the bathtub after Janet had beaten her. Now it was my turn, and I, too, though my skirt now covered my naked bottom, was shivering.

"Oh, God, help me," I prayed silently. "Forgive me for my transgressions and help me to submit to Thy will. Help me to be a better Christian." I couldn't understand why I had to be punished so much or so often to find His favor. "Dear God, how did I get to this place? What is happening? What have I done? Did I not help the Larrinagas when they were helpless? Did I not feed them when they were starving? Did I not clothe them when they wore rags for clothes? Was I not merciful and bore their burdens?" In my anguish I pondered these questions over and over. I could not understand why God reviled me, as Ron said He did. Sadly, I believed Ron wholeheartedly. I had lost the ability to think for myself, to question whether this man had, as he claimed, a direct line to God's thinking.

One day, My sister called to say Mom had been in a bad automobile accident and was in a coma. She wanted me to come to visit my mother. Ron refused permission. "Call her and tell her you are busy with your family duties and your duties to God, and she will have to take care of your mother herself," he ordered me. Crying, I obeyed. Mom died soon afterward, and Ron didn't allow me to attend her funeral, either. I never heard from anyone in my family again.

In my religious fervor, I felt we had a purpose, but even I could see it had only led us into pain and grief. Still, I reasoned, God must want us punished like this, or He wouldn't allow it to happen. Where had we gone wrong? What could we do to redeem ourselves in God's eyes? Despair overwhelmed me. Ron had gained control of not only our bodies, but our minds as well.

For a long time he had been taunting me, scolding me and the girls for what he called excessive modesty. "You teach your girls, especially Marian, to be abnormally modest around here! That is wrong! They are always pulling their dresses down to cover their legs and crossing their legs. We are their family! I am the servant of Jesus Christ. They have no need to be so modest before me. That is abnormal. You are abnormal!"

I was preoccupied with pulling myself and my family up from the depths of degradation in the eyes of God into which I had somehow fallen. Therefore, it was a great shock to me when Ron turned his sexual attention to me.

First, he created the perfect setting in which to work his conquest and overcome any objection to his evil purpose. Jack left the house early every morning to go to his teaching job, but Ron didn't work, so he was home all day. He'd sit with his Bible open in front of him, examining the Scriptures, going over, in minute detail, the conversation and actions of every person in the household, and anything and everything about the neighbors which Johnny or the boys reported to him. "I am the chosen servant of Jesus Christ," he'd proclaim over and over again, "specially chosen by God in this generation to be a light in the expanding darkness of Christian compromise!" If anyone asked him why he didn't work, he'd reply, "I can only fulfill my ministry, ordained by God, if given the opportunity to completely absorb myself in matters of the spiritual. I cannot concern myself with the material needs that occupy others. I must do only the Lord's work, to prevent compromise with the word of God."

Jack and I provided not just souls for him to save, but financial support for him and his entire extended family. That left him free to pursue his missionary work, and whatever else he chose to do. When we moved to the house in

Calmont, Jack had begun turning his paycheck over to Ron every two weeks when he received it. Not a penny of it went to us, but Ron assured us over and over that was the way God wanted it to be. "It is but a small sacrifice that will bring you far greater reward in Heaven than here on earth. You have a special part to play in a very important and significant plan that will have far-reaching implications in eternity," he informed us solemnly. "You are in a position to be eternally blessed if you surrender your material goods and give willingly what is needed to sustain the ministry and provide the material needs of our families. For that will allow me to continue in God's work."

I was not only willing, I was eager to do that. I wanted nothing so much as to gain such eternal blessing. I, and then Jack at my behest, followed all Ron's dictates. The others did the same. It not only gave us a sense of greater purpose, it inspired and compelled us to give all, and do all, so that Ron would be free of material cares and could devote himself to ministering to the needs of the ungodly. "I must increase the numbers that I convert to God's will," he told us, "and in that we will all receive God's blessings in eternity."

Not long after our new move, Ron began a campaign to isolate Jack from the rest of us. Although Jack obeyed him he had not become as deeply converted as I, and was not as malleable to Ron's will. That annoyed Ron, and he tried everything to gain better control over Jack. Since Jack went out every day and interacted with the real world, which the rest of us were not allowed to do, Jack was never totally under Ron's domination and control. Ron became determined to exert control over Jack's behavior at work as well as at home, and I felt, to a great extent, he eventually succeeded. He began to question Jack intensely each night about his every action, every minute he was not in class, and berate him for hours over any evidence he uncovered that Jack had associated with the "unsaved" outside of class. Jack would just sit there numbly and listen to Ron's harangues, head hung down, a guilty look on his face.

Then Ron would banish him to our room to "stay there alone and think about your sins. You are not worthy to associate with the rest of us, who do not compromise the word of God every day as you do out there with the heathen." He would not let Jack see the children, or have dinner with the other adults in the evenings. I was designated to deliver his meal in our room, scold him for his transgressions, and immediately report back to Ron anything Jack said in response. To get to me, Ron knew he had to somehow distance me even more, emotionally as well as physically, from Jack. So he humiliated Jack every night in some way and stepped up his attacks on Jack's failure to serve God the way Ron thought he should.

"You are not spiritually minded enough!" Ron challenged Jack when he came home each day. "You must go to your room and think about your interaction with the heathen, and about your commitment to God." Ron then gathered the rest of us around the table in the family room and lectured us about how Jack was offending God in going out and interacting with the heathen every day, and how he was disappointing God by refusing to follow God's will and teach only in Christian schools. In that way, Ron taught us to mock Jack, to question his motives, to lose our respect for him as a husband and father.

Gradually, insistently, he completely isolated Jack

from the rest of us. Then, suddenly, he forbade me to have any physical contact with my husband. "He is an outcast in the eyes of God. He is compromising God's word! You must not give him any comfort, physical or emotional, until he repents his ways! You must not sleep with him, or give him any physical satisfaction of your body. It is God's will that he be punished. You will confront him about his wickedness and interrogate him as to how he interacted with his unsaved students," Ron ordered.

If I felt Jack had been overly friendly, I was to reprimand him and coldly inform him he no longer had access to my body or my affection. If I didn't, I would be beaten by Ron, to whom I had to report our every word and who monitored everything we did. Whipped into subjugation mentally and physically, I followed Ron's orders.

Why did Jack accept such treatment? Why didn't he argue with me, or fight against it? That is a question I can't answer for him, except to say it seemed to me he was as much under Ron's domination as I was, though perhaps in a different way. Maybe he was just tired of fighting us. Maybe the humiliation and isolation had worked on him, too, and though he was a loving and good man, he believed, as I did, that we were sinners who needed to suffer in order to regain God's grace.

I only know I was too beaten and too under Ron's control to object to anything. The enforced separation of Jack from the rest of us went on for a long while, and that kind of isolation is as painful and effective as physical punishment. When Ron had succeeded in separating me from my husband, our closeness, and our marriage, were for all practical purposes destroyed.

We were people who truly wanted God's best for ourselves and our children. We didn't know we were following
a false prophet, who was filling us with lies and perverted
half-truths. I absolutely believed Ron with all my heart when
he said he was the chosen servant of Jesus Christ. I truly
believed we had somehow sinned against God and needed to
be punished to expiate those transgressions.

Finally, having separated me physically and emotionally from Jack, and having succeeded in dominating me in
every other way, Ron decided to take sexual control of me,
too.

One afternoon, he ordered me to accompany him to
the boys' bedroom, where I'd been sleeping in one of the
bunk beds, ever since Ron separated me from Jack's bed. My
knees shook with fear, for I thought I had done something
wrong and was in for another beating. Instead, he closed the
door quietly and spoke gently to me. That startled me. "I
brought you here to help you change, Mary. I want you to
have a better life. I hate to see you suffer so much, but you've
brought it all on yourself by being so rebellious. You mustn't
fight me, Mary. I'm here to help you, you know. You must
learn to be obedient to God's will and do what I ask, for I
know what is best for you. Will you do that?" I nodded yes.
He looked directly into my eyes and asked pleasantly, "Do
you want my help? Do you want to change so you can follow
the will of God for you?"

"Of course I do. You know that."

"Then you must also know that I do what I do in the
name of Jesus Christ to end the rebellion in your heart which
causes me to beat you." He called on me to remember how
an angry God destroyed the multitudes who challenged His

authority over their lives and also how God blessed those godly souls who followed his commandments. "You must accept that I am God's chosen servant, here to help you serve him. Don't you want your life to be better, don't you want to eat better, and enjoy your days?"

"Yes."

I hadn't eaten anything but cold cereal once a day for weeks, months, maybe almost a year. I had lost a lot of weight, and my clothes hung on me. "Do you want to go outside and enjoy the fresh air and sunshine?"

"Yes, of course I do."

"Then this is what you must do." He stared at me for a moment, then set his drink down on the little table next to the daybed. "Get undressed."

I must have just stared, I was so startled, so he said, "I want you to take off your clothes. All of them. Now." He couldn't mean what he was saying.

"No, I can't do that!" I protested, shock overcoming fear. "I'm a married woman."

"See? You are still rebellious!" His voice flashed in anger, then softened again. "Yes, you can," he said insistently, "and you must. You are cold to your husband, you shun his bed, he has told me so, and that's wrong. You have no right to deny him all the God-given pleasure you can."

"But . . ." I was stunned. Ron himself had demanded I quit Jack's bed and withhold sex from him!

"Be silent!" Now he was stern again, and I immediately subsided in fear. "God has commanded that I teach you how to relax and give a man pleasure. This is the only way you're going to loosen up and be normal. Sometimes the will of God is only accomplished through unorthodox means!

Remember, in Genesis, the continuance of Judah's line was accomplished only by his daughter-in-law dressing up as a harlot and seducing him in order to preserve spiritual seed in the will of God for the birth of Christ." He was breathing harder, and his blue eyes glittered at me. "Now, take off your clothes. If you can learn to undress in front of me, without modesty or shame, that will be the first step."

I didn't dare refuse him. There was certainly no sexual desire in me. Hungry and compliant, like Janet and all the kids, I was little more than Ron's robot, terrified of punishment, willing to do anything to avoid beatings and isolation.

I knew what I would have to do. I knew Ron intended to have sex with me and would brook no refusal from me. On another, more animal level, I really didn't care, if it would mean better conditions, fewer beatings, and more food for me. I was caught in a love-hate relationship with Ron and had been from the beginning. This was only one more aspect of the tangled emotional state into which he had slowly, inexorably, drawn me.

In truth, I had no choice. He could brutally rape me, and no one would come to my aid. But he was excusing his intentions by telling me that it was the will of God that I voluntarily give myself to him! "Well?" He was getting impatient. "Will you take them off, or will your rebellion persist until I have to have Kathleen come in and strip you naked and beat you into submission?" I knew he'd do it, too.

Slowly, my hands shaking, I began to remove my clothes. I prayed someone would come in and interrupt, but he had planned his moment well. He'd sent Janet and the other adults to the store, and the kids were with Kathleen at the other side of the house for a long Bible study lesson. Jack was at school and wouldn't be home for hours.

I unbuttoned my blouse and slid it off. Ron never took his eyes off me. "Continue," was all he said when I hesitated. "You must overcome this excessively false modesty, Mary." I unbuttoned my skirt and stepped out of it. I carefully folded it, like a tidy housewife, and laid it on one of the bunk beds. I have always been extremely modest and fastidious by nature and had never had to undress in this way in front of any man, not even Jack. It was the most degrading and humiliating experience I had ever endured, this strip tease I was being forced to perform for Ron. He waited, saying nothing, and I pulled my slip off over my head. "Just drop it on the floor," he said impatiently, "and get the rest off! Hurry up. I've seen your bare bottom before, you know, when Kathleen is disciplining you." My face flamed. He'd be more than glad to do it again now, his look told me clearly, if I didn't obey and get my clothes off. Hurriedly, I removed my bra and pants and stood there completely naked and exposed.

"Don't look away, look at me," he commanded. I hated that moment and could feel a blush searing my whole body. I had bruises here and there and felt shameful and ugly. He had told me again and again how awful I was, what a harlot I was. I didn't want anyone to look at me, ever, and certainly not him. I shivered. Ron grabbed my upper arm and pulled me close, then put both his arms around me. Then he gently turned me facing away from him and ran his hands lightly down my back and over my buttocks. He had not taken his clothes off and that made me feel even more naked and vulnerable. I was shaking uncontrollably. "Lay down on the bed and calm yourself," he ordered. Obediently, I crawled onto the day bed near the window and lay there, waiting. He stretched out beside me, but didn't remove his clothes.

He began to stroke my hair and body and to talk softly to me. "See. You can do it. You can take off your clothes and be a normal woman. You can give up that false modesty, which is not necessary in this house. I am here to help you, to teach you. Now try to relax. I'm not going to hurt you, if you turn yourself to God's will for you and allow me to show you how a woman gives pleasure."

With that, he drew even closer and began to fondle my breasts, his hand sliding down over my belly. When he reached between my legs, I jumped, tensing, trying to pull away. "Please don't," I whimpered. "I can't do this."

"Yes, you can. You must trust me. Don't tense up, relax," he said. "There, that's it, that's right," he was murmuring to me in that deep hypnotic voice of his. "Good, good. Submit yourself to the Lord in this, and you will be helped by Him." He began getting out of his clothes but had to leave me and get up to take them off. I turned away, so I wouldn't have to look at him. He climbed back into bed and began touching and stroking me everywhere, then suddenly brutally forced his fingers inside me. I cried out. My back arched from the pain, and I tried to pull away. "Relax," he ordered again, this time harshly. "I am going to stimulate you." I was still dry, and it hurt, but I bit my lip to keep from crying out again. He was fully aroused and rolled on top of me and tried to enter me. I was so thin my hip bones and pelvic bones stuck out. "Relax and bend your knees," he commanded. "Your bones are sticking into me and hurting me. You're not very comfortable for a man's pleasure. We'll have to put more flesh on these bones." I closed my eyes and prayed for it to be over with, and soon enough it was. Satisfied, Ron rolled off me and got dressed. "See, you can be a normal woman," he said to me. "You can learn to pleasure a man as you should, without false modesty. I will continue to help you in this way. Now, get dressed and go back to your duties in the kitchen." He picked up his drink again and promptly left the room, closing the door firmly behind him.

I lay there, my mind spinning. I felt dirty, used, cast off. I dared not cry out loud, but I cried inside. What we had just done was a sin, and I knew deep inside it was wrong, no matter what Ron said. He allowed no compromise with God's word as Ron spoke it. But it was contrary to God's word for a married woman to have sex with a man other than her husband, and I knew that. Somehow, though, Ron managed to twist God's word to whatever his purpose was and to support him as right in everything he said and did. If I dared even question him, which I was deathly afraid to do, he'd show me quotations from Scripture to justify what he had just done. But what he had done was rape me, as surely as if I had been bound and gagged and taken at knife point.

After that, Ron continued his afternoon sex sessions with me in the boys' room several times a week, and I began getting better meals. "Feed her more and fatten her up some, for she is skin and bones, a disgrace in the eyes of the Lord." Kathleen, with a knowing smirk, piled food on my plate at mealtimes. Then she'd watch over me like a guard dog to see that I ate it all. I was used to eating very little, so at first what she put on my plate made me ill. I would throw up after eating so much more than I was used to. Then Kathleen would take me into the next room and beat me soundly for "wasting God's bounty," and Ron watched while she did it, but didn't interfere. Many of the beatings came right after lunch, and soon afterward he'd order me to the boys' room with him again, and he'd be so aroused from watching Kathleen whip me on my bare bottom that he'd barely wait for me to get my clothes off before he fell on me. Soon I was able to eat more and keep it down, and I began gaining back some weight. There were fewer beatings. That raised false hope in me.

Ron was soon obsessed with his sexual interest in me. He wanted me constantly. He sent Randall, Johnny, Janet, and the others out more often to get food and made Kathleen take the kids to the other end of the house. He'd send the older boys out to do yard work, and then he would take me to his own room to continue his "lessons," teaching me, he said, how to be a "normal woman, free of false and immoral modesty, as God intended." He became more creative in the ways in which he had sex with me, always making me strip in front of him first, forcing me to have oral sex and to assume various submissive positions. He never suggested that I was cured enough, or "normal enough," though, to go back to having sex with Jack, my own husband.

Sometimes Ron would steal quietly into my room in the early morning. Jimmy or one of the other younger boys would still be in bed asleep, but that didn't stop Ron when he was aroused. He just came in, climbed in with me, and paid no attention to whether or not the kids could see him. Sometimes I thought he even hoped they were watching—that made him more aroused. But then I prayed to God to forgive me for having such evil thoughts against His chosen servant. "Help me to learn, God, help me to be less modest, and to overcome my rebellious mind," I'd pray. I had no desire except somehow to please Ron, and by pleasing him to earn points with God.

As weeks passed, Janet became suspicious and began to resist going out to shop in the afternoons. Though normally he didn't care what he did or what anyone else in the family saw, Ron did try to conceal what he was doing with me from Janet and Jack. I was terrified that they'd find out and so ashamed I would never have breathed a word to anyone.

When Janet stubbornly refused to leave in the afternoons, Ron began sending me out to the back yard late in the evening, after supper, to water the plants and flowers we were growing on the hillside in the back. At first, I was glad for the opportunity, because I hadn't been allowed outside much in over a year. Watering that hillside was a major project. We had hundreds of flowering plants and vegetables growing back there, and they had to be watered at least six inches deep in order to grow. Water would come cascading down the hill, and dirt and mud with it, and I'd be dirty and soaking wet in no time. Ron would send Johnny or one of the older kids out to check on whether or not I'd done the job right. They'd poke a finger into the dirt here and there, and, if the soil wasn't wet to a depth of five or six inches, I would be taken in and Ron would then personally beat me on my bare bottom, with his hand, or his own belt. Then he'd send me back outside to water again. "I'll be there soon to inspect," he'd warn darkly.

"I'm going up there," he'd announce a few minutes later to Janet and the others, "to check on whether that worthless harlot has done the job right this time!" After a while, I recognized his footsteps coming up the path. It was completely dark, and he'd come quietly up behind me and grab me, pulling me against him, his hardness pressing against my buttocks, his hands on my breasts. "Turn off the nozzle and put the hose down," he'd whisper hoarsely in my ear. I could smell the heavy, sharp smell of whiskey on his breath. Then he'd sway me back and forth against him, rubbing himself hard against my damp body. If I stiffened, or tried to pull away, he'd turn me and pull up my dress and slap my rear hard, scolding me in a fierce whisper. "Why do you continue to fight me? Why can't you just learn to submit? You are rebellious! Accept the will of God for your benefit!" Crying, I'd force myself to hold still, to relax, to let him do whatever he wanted to me. He'd turn me facing away from him and lift my wet skirt in back, pulling down my panties, and running his fingers between my legs in back. "Bend forward," he'd say, and I'd obediently bend, and he'd take me that way, standing there, his hands kneading my breasts as he thrust into me roughly from behind.

I dared not make a sound, and all I ever heard was his harsh breath coming faster and faster. Our garden escapades were safely hidden from the house and any spying neighbors under the dark blanket of the night sky. I was relieved that he always satisfied himself quickly those times. Then he'd push me away and carefully rearrange his clothes, then mine. Then, loudly, he'd say, "You didn't get it wet deep enough! Stupid, wicked woman! Can't you learn these plants need plenty of water? Continue watering until the job is done right, or you'll be severely punished for your transgressions!"

After he had gone back to the house, I allowed myself a sigh of despair as I resumed watering. He had long since abandoned all pretense of "teaching" me anything that would please God. Now he openly used me for his pleasure, whenever and however he chose to do so, and I numbly submitted to whatever he wanted me to do.

But Janet was not as unobservant as he had thought. Before too long, they were fighting bitterly over Ron's "close supervision" of my watering tasks. Up there in the garden, I could hear them clearly through an open window. "What were you doing out there so long?" Janet would shout, when he went back in. "How long can it take to check on watering! Where is *she*?" Then she'd start screaming at him, "You just went up there to be with *her*, I know! What are you two doing out there in the dark! I've seen your eyes on her and how you look at her. You're not fooling me for a minute!"

"Silence, woman! Are you questioning me?" Ron would shout back. Then sounds of a scuffle, heavy smacks, and Janet screaming in pain. "Dare you challenge your husband? I answer only to Jesus Christ, not to you!" From the sounds, I knew he'd taken off his belt and was whaling her with it. It would smack her bare flesh, and she'd cry and beg him to stop like we all did when we were being beaten, and, when he had her sobbing and subdued, he'd call the kids in. "Look! Look here at your wicked, wanton mother! She is challenging and accusing her husband, the chosen servant of Jesus Christ! Look what a harlot you have for a mother! She is rebellious and does not submit her will to her husband! She must learn to submit. She must be punished."

The children knew their role. "Yes," they would say. "He has done nothing wrong! You are rebellious. He is serving the will of God. You must be submissive to him, wicked woman!" And having scolded and denied their mother and defended Ron, they would be allowed to go out. Then Ron would hit Janet a couple of more times with the belt, for good measure, and leave her there, sobbing. I knew I'd get the same treatment if I dared to challenge him.

"Oh, God," I prayed earnestly, "help me to submit my will. Show me a ray of light."

After that, Ron became more careless about his behavior with me when the little children and Janet were around. It was almost as if he was daring them to notice, or object. But they knew that the result of that would be more beatings and punishment, so they dutifully kept silent, and turned their eyes and ears away. He was always careful, though, to keep what he was doing to me secret from the older boys, and from Jack.

5

the back of fools

It was there in Tartola, too, that Ron became the intent overseer of what he claimed were our United States Constitutional rights. During the day, and in the evenings, he'd subject us to long-winded lectures about the history of religious freedom and the terrible religious persecution of our forbears. "Our ancestors," he'd proclaim, "were forced to flee England and Europe to find the promised land in America, where they were free to worship God in peace and according to the dictates of conscience, rather than having to follow the preconceived ideas of the European churches. Fortunately, we still have the freedom to worship God as we choose here. We must let no one interfere with our adherence to the word of God!"

A lot of his teaching and instruction were now focused on how we were to act to outwit and evade the police, school officials, or nosy neighbors, actually anyone who might pose a threat, real or imagined, to our lives together as "loving, Christ-dedicated Christian families." Ron traveled less in the motor home to do missionary work, as he had done in the years before we moved to Tartola.

However, whenever they went away and then came back for rest, money, and fresh food supplies, Ron always had tales of how God the Holy Spirit had warned him of impending danger, and how God miraculously helped him escape the clutches of the police, who, he insisted, were "bent on depriving all of us of our religious freedom and our constitutional rights." He had managed, miraculously, to escape the clutches of the police on numerous occasions. He had learned on those occasions, and now he carefully taught us, how to barrage them with accusations, with lawsuits, with standoffs, with letters, with recriminations. Jack and I, or Kathleen and I, or Johnny and I, had to type, record, and mail out scores of letters to every authority from local to federal level whenever Ron went on one of his rampages against the police or the school authorities. If we failed to succeed in calling them off, if we failed in our duty to bring to their attention all the legal ramifications that, according to Ron, "abuse of our religious freedom and constitutional rights will incur," to quote one of the lines he most frequently used, then we were severely punished: beaten, harangued, denied food, and humiliated. Jack and I, Johnny and Kathleen suffered the most in these endeavors, because we were the ones designated by Ron to be the household secretaries and typists.

Ron Larrinaga told us that God had formed him in the womb to be the spokesman to this generation of what he termed "compromising Christians, who have sacrificed and abandoned their sacred trust from God to hold true to the disciplined doctrines of Scripture." In California, Ron Larrinaga believed he'd found his Promised Land.

Ron always emphatically pointed out what a terrible sin compromise of any sort was, or any deviation from the exact written word of God as represented by the Scriptures. He interpreted their meaning to us, for that, he told us, was his mission as the chosen servant of Jesus Christ. God, he continually threatened, could in a matter of seconds throw down kingdoms and mighty kings who opposed His word. Whenever Ron quoted these verses from the Old Testament, they were like arrows to my heart. Did not God say in Deuteronomy, "I set before thee life and death, blessing and cursing, therefore choose life that both thee and thy seed shall live?" To me, all that I did in following Ron became the way to continue life as God commanded it.

I accepted the torment and torture and suffering he inflicted on me, and on my children, as something we deserved, and the others seemed to me to do the same, because it was done with Scriptural quotations that illustrated the need for it as commanded by God, and justified it. "Chasten thy son while there is hope," Ron would quote when ordering the children beaten, or when beating them himself, "and let not thy soul spare for his crying."

He would add, "Judgments are prepared for scorners, and stripes for the backs of fools." We got plenty of stripes, from his belt, from hairbrushes, from switches, from belts stripped into cat-o-nine tails, from branches. He made sure we understood and accepted this torture because we had somehow sinned and were therefore little more than "fools and scorners" in the eyes of God. We must pay for that, or remain distanced from God's acceptance and love.

We learned to endure terrible beatings, counting the strokes, blanking out our minds to everything except getting through it alive. We were literally flayed, over and over again, until blood spattered the walls from our wounds and great purple welts were raised on our bodies. Gradually, we came to believe and accept what was pounded into us day and night, day in and day out.

Jack and I had little or no contact with the outside world to dispute Ron's theories. We were completely cut off from our families and from all interaction with the world outside our private enclave. Ron's perverted view of life and of God's will became our daily norm. Only Jack went out to work, and he was interrogated minutely, and punished severely, for any interaction with anyone outside of class. He was forbidden to speak to others, except on school business, and was never able to discuss our life at home on pain of terrible punishment. "For they are the heathen, who would lead you on the path of Satan and would understand nothing of our Christian life." By then, Ron Larrinaga's spiritual and emotional control over us all was total. We had forsaken our families and our friends to follow him. We believed in him as our only way to win the love of Jesus Christ. We obeyed him as slaves obey a master, for the retribution if we displeased him was swift and terrible.

During this period, Ron's son Randall was spared the worst punishments, for, with greater responsibility—and Randall bore heavy responsibilities in that family—came greater privilege. However, when he reached his late teens he had the normal urges of a growing adolescent. That was swiftly and severely scotched by Ron. One day, I overheard Ron accusing Randall of having an "illicit interest" in Marian, my daughter. Marian was developing into a lovely young teenager and was strikingly sweet in personality. "You must not look at her, or speak to her!" said Ron. "Your place is to do God's will and perform your duties to the family. You have no business thinking about women! You are to cleanse your mind of such impure thoughts and give yourself wholly to God. Only when you do that will God help you to conquer all sexual desire."

I had to wonder at that, since Ron had made no effort to conquer his own sexual desires where I was concerned. I didn't know that he was also preying on the girls. If there were any outward signs of Ron's aberrant sexual behavior toward his own children or mine, I hadn't noticed them. Maybe I had seen things that seemed unusual to me, but, like accepting the rationale for the beatings and other punishments, I had just buried it all so I wouldn't have to think about it. Ron's daughters, like mine, were all pretty, with long blonde hair and nice figures. Ruth, Sheila, Hannah, and Dana were now all in their teens, but had never gone to school and did none of the normal things children their age did. They were never permitted to talk to any of our boys without Ron's personal supervision, nor did they have any friends outside our home. None of them so much as made a phone call to anyone outside our family.

Rigidly and strictly, Ron controlled and lectured all the children about sex, sexual deviation, or any interaction not ordained by God, while he frequently broke all those laws of God himself. He would beat the boys terribly if they so much as glanced at the bathroom door when one of the girls went in. Once, he found one of the boy's underpants in a drawer with what he believed were semen stains on them, and that was fodder for a terrible whipping for the offender, before everyone, and then a long session of public humiliation, with the underpants on his head, as had been done to me when I had lost control and wet my pants during a beating.

Because of his strict, rigid stance about sex, I would never have believed Ron would sexually abuse the children, or force me into deviate sex with him against my will, but I was wrong about that, as I was wrong about so many things. One day, when he had me in the children's room, where there were bunk beds, he made me sit on the bottom bunk and perform oral sex on him. He was standing, and he had one of his daughters lying there on the top bunk. As he'd push into my mouth, holding my head with my hair wrapped in his one hand, pulling it, he was abusing her sexually with his fingers, talking to her about how she was being good and "doing God's will for you." After that, he took to keeping one of the children in the room when he was having sex with me, because he knew it upset them and humiliated me.

The times when Ron traveled in the motor home to do missionary work became the only times we got some respite from the terrible physical punishment he called down upon our heads, especially when he was drinking heavily. When he went on those trips, he'd take Janet and Johnny along, but would usually leave Kathleen behind to maintain discipline. We knew our every action was spied upon and would be reported to Ron on his return, but it wasn't as bad as when he was there to mete out punishments himself. The children played, we were able to relax a little, and even shared an occasional laugh. It never occurred to any of us to leave, to call in the authorities, or to try to escape. This was a measure of how complete his mind control over all of us was.

On one trip, Ron insisted on taking Marian along with him. His son Randall also went with them. It was probably on that trip that Ron made his first sexual advances on Marian, and may have even forced her to submit to him, as he had me and the other older girls, raping her, and Randall knew about what his father had done to Marian. But it wasn't until all those years later that he was able to speak about it.

While on that same trip, Ron called and ordered us to put my son Philip on a bus to join him. He had for a long time been accusing Philip of being "rebellious and uncooperative with the word of God."

He said on the phone, "I am going to take measures to bring Philip into obedience with God." That struck fear into my heart, but I did not dare to refuse to obey. Philip departed, and, when he arrived at where they were staying, Ron told him he had decided it was necessary for Philip to leave and join the armed services. "You are rebellious and must learn to mature and live with the nature of your decisions." Philip was scared and upset about leaving the family. He reluctantly obeyed Ron's wishes. "You are to send every paycheck home to me," Ron ordered, "so that I can continue to do God's work. I will send you money every month for your basic needs." Initially, out from under Ron's control, Philip rebelled. But Ron went quickly to the base where Philip was stationed and convinced him that he was being a terrible sinner and needed to atone at once or God would strike him dead. Philip was still controlled by Ron, and he truly believed God might strike him dead, so he began sending his paychecks home to Ron. For the first few months, Ron continually followed Philip from base to base across the country, using the motor home, to keep tabs on him. That way, he was able to keep him in line with his religious doctrine. It was very successful. Philip eventually became a model disciple for Ron, even though he was now out in the world.

Meanwhile, little Ellen's punishment from Ron increased. All the children were punished severely for various infractions, but now Ron's rage suddenly seemed to fall on hapless little Ellen. She had a weak bladder, and, ever since she was a toddler, she was made to stand in a corner while they fed her water, then demanded she hold her urine and not wet herself. "She must learn to control her body and to obey." The poor little kid would jump around trying to hold it, but she would start crying and then wet herself. After which, Kathleen or Ron or one of the Millers would beat her terribly. How awful that was! It drove me nearly crazy. Once, in a rage because I had protested him beating Ellen so hard, Ron ordered all the children to go and urinate in the toilet. Then, grabbing my hair, he dunked my head down into the urine filled toilet in front of them all, shouting, "See, see! She is the mother and does not control the child! See how God wills that she be punished by the children!" The children just stared, round-eyed, and nodded their heads, Yes.

As I came up choking and gagging, my eyes burning from the urine, Ellen screamed and cried in stark terror. Little as she was, she knew that somehow she had been the cause of my punishment, and it must have hurt and frightened her terribly. I'd try to comfort her, but I was kept from her. Sometimes, too, she'd try to comfort me. If I was standing in a corner, or lying in the closet after a beating, she'd come sit by me with her little coloring book and crayons, and she'd pat me and say, "Don't cry, Mommy, don't cry."

It was about that time that Ron decided that Louise, too, had grown "too rebellious" as she grew older. Ron began ostracizing her from the rest of us, punishing her severely.

Then he'd isolate Jack and me, too, but in separate areas of the house, making everyone else shun us as "parents who cannot properly control their wicked, rebellious daughter." When Louise did not repent, as he demanded, he announced to us one day, "It is necessary and important for her welfare, since she refuses to repent, that she be exposed to the world, so she will better appreciate what she has here, in the will of God." Then he would beat Louise unmercifully, again and again, then make me beat her, trying to bring her to repentance. Nothing worked. Finally, he confined her to a closet, where she remained for a long time, allowed out only to eat something, to be beaten, or to go to the bathroom.

Now Ron segregated Louise from the other members of the family, and, when not working, she was made to stand or sit in a closet. Her internment in a corner or closet grew to hours, days, weeks, months, and continued for a year and a half. During that period, she tried very hard to please God. She prayed and prayed, desperately seeking the transformation Ron wanted. When Ron saw no evidence of the demanded metamorphosis, he compared her to Esau, saying she had somehow sold her birthright and was evil. Though she repented, praying to be saved, he condemned her.

Occasionally she was let out and examined "to see if you have a change of attitude," Ron would say. But, according to him, she hadn't. I watched as Louise withdrew into her mind where no one could reach her. Most of the time, she seemed to live in a distant fantasy world, blankly ignoring our external reality. While she survived by internalizing, she was by no means insane. Occasionally her face mirrored the horror of her and our painful predicament.

Finally, Ron convinced me that it was important to get

Louise out of the house before she infected everyone else with her sins. Therefore, he said, Louise must go into the service. When she left home, Ron told her, "If you don't change your ways and repent, God will kill you within a few months."

Louise was not as docile, or as heavily under Ron's influence as Philip was. "I kept waiting for God to strike me dead," Louise wrote back, "and was very surprised when, six months later, I was still very much alive." After that, Louise quit writing or sending money home and cut all her ties with us. After a year or two, she wrote to me to tell us she was married and had a child. I never saw the letter. It was confiscated by Ron, who read it and then confronted Jack. Ron was furious that Louise had dared to marry at all, never mind that she did so without first seeking his permission. As punishment, we were ordered to completely shun her, and to deny her as our daughter. I was heartbroken. Jack was told by Ron to write and tell her she was no longer part of our family.

"She is an evil, wicked, whorish woman!" Ron said.

That letter, written by Jack, was one of the most heart-wrenching letters ever penned by a father to his daughter. I was required by Ron to make a copy of it and to keep that copy in our household files, where we kept copies of everything. When I think of what it must have done to Louise's heart, it brings a flood of tears to my eyes. The handwritten diatribe, complete with Scriptural quotations—just like Ron—went on for pages. Jack was trying to impress Ron with how well he had learned. It concluded with a damnation of Louise for the wickedness and whoredom and his banning her from writing to or having anything to do with any member of the family.

After that, we didn't hear from Louise again.

Ron jumped on that incident to punish me as the "whore mother who had neither raised her daughter in the love of Christ, nor with respect to His word!" I was beaten severely with a belt. Whenever her name came up, he'd say, "That whore of a daughter of hers!" Then he'd point at me and say to Kathleen, "Take her and beat her until she can't stand!" The beatings went on almost daily and were excruciating. But it wasn't only the beatings. Ron thought of everything possible he could do to me to make my life miserable. He cut my food down to nearly nothing: broth, water, sometimes corn meal and rice, a bit of cold cereal. I lost weight, and weakened.

Then, one by one, he began to isolate my two other older children, though I was in too much of a daze to even realize that was what he was doing. He had neutralized Jack, and Philip was in the armed service. I was his obedient slave. He had lost Louise, and now turned on Marian and David. Marian was isolated, and David was put in charge of watching her and reporting on her every move. At times, he had to beat her, and he was also ordered by Ron to beat me, his own mother. Marian was beaten constantly, and she was completely restricted to a small area of the house. She wasn't allowed to talk to any of us, or eat with us. I, too, was restricted, for being her mother. I was kept in the bedroom opposite to her, or in the corner of the hallway. I could hear Marian's heartbroken, despairing sobbing from the other bedroom. One night, I chanced sneaking into her room to try to comfort her, and she was afraid to even have my hand touch her, because she was fearful that Ron would come in and catch us, and we would both be beaten unmercifully again.

A few days later, Jack appeared on our side of the house, stone-faced. "Marian, you are to come with me today," he said. "Pack up your things." She obediently packed her few belongings and was crying when she left with her father. When he came back, alone, I was told that Marian, too, would not be back. "She is to work in the world and earn her way and send money to us for our Christian mission," said Ron. My heart sank. For the first month or two, Marian obediently sent her paycheck home, as Philip did, but then one day she wrote Ron that she needed her money to buy art supplies and wondered if that would be all right. "Art supplies!" Ron snorted. He immediately wrote her and refused permission, saying, "You're a wicked, greedy young woman! You are more interested in yourself and art than in honoring Christ and your family in an evil, wicked world!"

The next day, Ron told us, "I'm going to go and personally talk to Marian. She must be brought back into the fold and understanding God's will for her life." I don't know what happened between them on that visit, but soon after that Marian came home for a brief period. I was kept in the kitchen doing the dishes, or in my room. I wasn't permitted any direct contact or conversation with my daughter. But I remember that one night she and Ron were in the hallway, adjacent to the kitchen, while I was doing the dishes. He was verbally attacking her, as he had all of us women many times before, for her "false modesty." He reprimanded her for crossing her legs and acting weird and being overly protective of her body. Then he turned suddenly and glared down the hall at me. I shivered. "Look at your mother down there!" he said, pointing at me accusingly. "She is at fault! She has never treated your sexuality in a normal way. You must learn to be normal. You will never be allowed to come home again if you continue this rebellious behavior!" He had his face close to hers, eyeball to eyeball, and Marian was shaking and trembling, and her eyes were full of tears. Then he ordered me beaten by Kathleen for teaching excessive modesty to my daughters, and he personally beat Marian with his belt until she was screaming. She left shortly after that. Sixteen-year-old David became Ron's next target.

After Louise, Philip, and Marian were sent away, David had to prove to Ron that he was capable of taking his place with the older boys in order to forestall continual beatings. He was a skinny little kid, who looked years younger than his actual age.

A few months later, Ron caught him peeing in the yard outside, something all the boys, and Ron himself, did often when they were out there working. Ron made a big case of it, beating David terribly, holding him up to shame and humiliation and ridicule before all of us, as was his practice. Then Ron sent him away. I wondered why he didn't send his own children or Johnny or Kathleen, why it was always my kids who had to leave.

Meanwhile, my other children faced pain of another kind. When Jimmy was in the room and Ron decided he wanted sex with me, he didn't send Jimmy out. "Turn around!" he'd order him. "Don't be looking at your mother." Then he would assault me with his hands and body, as poor little Jimmy stood there, facing the wall of the bedroom, mortified. Jimmy told me, much later, that he had also seen Ron having sexual intercourse with one of his own daughters.

Often Ellen, who was only seven then, was around

when Ron wanted to have sex with me. He would tell her not to look, though he'd allow her to leave the room if she wanted to. "Turn around and mind your own business," he'd say, "or go in the other room and play." Then he'd shut my bedroom door and have me to himself.

6

hate thy neighbor

Relations with our neighbors bordered on warfare, and for once Ron didn't run away. When he decided he would fight a battle instead of running away from it as he usually did, he was a formidable opponent. The neighbors and police soon discovered how formidable.

When the neighbors on the street above us first complained to us about the music and the noise, Ron was furious that they dared to try and interfere with him. "Heathens, complaining of the way a decent Christian family lives in service to God every day!" he would shout at them when they came to the door. "Better that you look to your own souls and the will of God in your lives!" Then he'd quote some long passage of Scripture at them. Frustrated, they'd slink away home. Ron would then turn the outside loud-speakers toward the location of the home of the complainer. He'd play music at top volume and preach at them at the top of his voice, calling them "whores, sinners, and heathens," shouting, "You're all ungodly perverts who are going straight to hell!" Within a year, the petty insults and confrontations between Ron and our neighbors had mounted to a crescendo, and then the formal complaints began.

When the neighbors called the police about us, they claimed there was continual "disturbance of the peace" at our house. Ron played loud music over the intercom system and had the older boys use power tools until all hours to cover the sounds of screaming and crying when the rest of us were being "disciplined." Also, the boys had begun work building a carport into the side of the hill next to the house, which would garage the motor home. Ron wanted it built so we could back the motor home into it, facing out, so he could get out quickly if he had to.

Once the neighbors filed complaints with the police, we immediately filed counter complaints, claiming "religious harassment, denial of our religious freedom, and abridgement of our constitutional rights." The complaints and counter complaints to the police became so numerous that they were finally summed up by one police officer by a single cryptic comment, "An ongoing neighbor dispute over every petty issue in existence."

The neighbors knew something strange and unsavory was going on at our house, and they tried repeatedly to get the police involved. However, the police, wary of our insistence that the neighbors were creating "infringement of our constitutional rights" and "interference with our right to worship God in peace in our Christian home," rarely ventured beyond the yard or front door to investigate. We usually succeeded in keeping them out. The first time they did come in, Ron was ready for them. He knew exactly how to behave, and he'd taught us exactly how to appear and act when any authority showed up to question us.

"Come in, officers, and see for yourselves," he invited them cordially, smiling expansively. "We're a fine Christian family. This is Mr. Rich, a teacher in our public schools," he said, introducing Jack. "And these are our children." Kathleen and I had hastily dressed and scrubbed up a few of the children, never more than three or four. Dressed in long-sleeved dresses and shirts to cover any telltale bruises, the children presented themselves shyly to the police, and did not speak unless spoken to. "I am a minister of the gospel of Jesus Christ," Ron informed the officers. "I graduated from State College of the Bible, and my friend here," he'd say, pointing to Jack, "has a master's degree in science. The others are similarly educated," he'd add as Johnny Spencer and Kathleen Miller nodded in agreement. "We're informed, we're intelligent, and we're concerned Americans, and these people who complain are just harassing us and trying to deny us our constitutional rights. They are unwilling to let a good Christian family live in peace to follow the word of the Lord. It is they who should be punished and locked up."

Some of the officers who came were as impressed as Ron intended them to be, and immediately left. Others were more skeptical, especially as time dragged on and the complaints increased. They often acted rudely. They got very tired of investigating yet another complaint against us. However, we knew how to deal with their hostility, too. We'd immediately hit the typewriter, and off would go letters to every authority above them, expressing indignation about their treatment of us and their constant interference in our Christian lives.

We were confident of our command of English and

our ability to write intelligent letters, and we didn't hesitate to call on the FBI and even the President of the United States for help. At one point, we formally charged the police department with "conspiracy to deny us our right to live according to the dictates of our conscience, in peace." The California Justice Department came to our house twice to investigate those charges.

Excerpts from police reports and notes I was required to type up for Ron show how things went between us and our neighbors during that period:

• Neighbor called police and reported a ridiculous charge of hammer banging in the night. The police arrived at two o'clock. We met Officer Tate in our night clothes at the front door. We told him to go away, we were asleep and no one was banging hammers, so he went away to a neighbor's and returned fifteen minutes later with a long list of accusations, changing the charge of hammer banging to loud playing of music at all hours.

• Neighbor called complaining of loud music, like a party. Officer Gross was angry with us. We met him in our night clothes at the door and told him we were asleep, he had awakened us, and that we are Christians and don't party.

• Neighbor called the police again on a charge of loud music at midnight. Officers came, but when we invited them to come into our living room, they could find no evidence of a party going on. They apologized and left.

• Neighbor blocked the entrance to our street with his vehicle and challenged us to dare to try to pass.

• Neighbors called police. Officer Tate came. A contractor was here running a cement mixer. You couldn't have heard a radio for all the noise of building our carport. The officer abused us and violated all our civil rights.

• Officer Tate was observed on the street above us in a patrol car, making a surveillance of us as we were in the back yard.

We called the police department to inquire about illegal surveillance of us and were told that Officer Tate was off duty.
• Neighbor from the street above screamed down at us, cursing, then called police to report on us. Police responded to
them in two squad cars at 6:30 p.m. They piled out of their
cars and said, "What are you guys doing here?" We told them
we were only talking in our own yard. We told them we were
living as peaceful Christian families, and the neighbors were
persecuting us.

In the complaint that instigated that last report, Ron
had actually been preaching at the neighbors in a loud voice,
berating them and exhorting them to submit to God's will for
them.

In June, we received a letter back from the police
chief, replying to our formal complaint. "I can assure you,"
he wrote, "that a conspiracy between your neighbors and
officers of the Department to harass and persecute you, members of your family, and friends, does not exist. I very much
regret you have that perception."

That only served to aggravate Ron further, and he
gave me a sound beating for not making my letter to the
authorities convincing enough. It went on like that, month in
and month out, for two years. Eventually, the police became
sick of us, and we of them.

Meanwhile, the terrible beatings and the sexual and
emotional abuse of all of us continued. So did the humilia-
tions. One day, when I demurred at performing a sex act he
wanted, Ron grabbed me by my long hair and, yanking me
off my feet, dragged me along the floor to the bathroom. "On
your knees, harlot!" he ordered, kicking me brutally. I
screamed in pain, and he shoved my head down into the toi-

let, nearly strangling me, and then flushed it. My hair was pulled down with the water flushing out, and tangled there. I screamed in pain and terror, feeling as though my hair was being ripped right out of my head, and my scalp with it. Finally, Ron yanked my head out, leaving some of my hair behind. "See how God punishes the wicked and disobedient woman?" he yelled. "You are a whore, a rebellious harlot, and you shall be punished!" He threw me aside, and I staggered against the wall and collapsed on the floor, sobbing hysterically, my wet hair dripping in a puddle around me.

I prayed, "God, kill me, just take me to hell now."

"Clean yourself up and clean that mess up. Then go to the corner in the hall and repent!" Ron ordered. "I want nothing of you now, nothing! You are a wicked harlot, do you understand?" I could only nod and whimper.

Ron hated one of our neighbors in particular, Ted Baker. He'd shout insults at him every time he saw him, like, "Pervert!" and "Christ-rejecter!" and "Heathen!" as Baker drove up the hill to his home. Finally, Baker came to the end of his rope with Ron's insults. He'd been drinking heavily, and he went into his house, got out his repeating pistol and a shotgun, drove down the hill to near our house, and waited at the foot of the road, guns at the ready, for Ron to appear. He turned his truck crosswise to block the roadway into our house. When Ron's car finally came up the hill, Randall was in it, not Ron. Randall stopped to see what was going on, and Baker opened fire on him! It's a miracle he didn't kill Randall, but fortunately the first shots missed.

Hollering, "Hold it! What the hell?" Randall dived under the car and wiggled to the other side for protection.

We heard the gunshots and Randall's shout up at the

house. Ron ran for his guns. He handed the guns to Jack and the older boys. "Here. Use these if necessary. Jack! Go down there and see what's going on!" Ron wasn't about to risk his own hide. Jack started down toward the action, and Baker began firing at him. Three or four shots rang out, and Jack jumped behind a tree, a bullet narrowly missing his head. Drunk out of his mind and completely enraged, Baker just kept firing. We were looking out the front window and could see the whole thing. I was terrified, and so were the children.

Ron called the police. "Hurry! Our neighbor is shooting at us, trying to kill us!" The cops came tearing up the hill again, sirens screaming, and, as soon as he heard them, Ron called for Jack to come in. "Give me the guns! Quick!" he said and locked his guns away. Then he went out and watched as they arrested Baker, who was still sitting there with his gun, and took him away. Ron finally had the leverage he needed, or so he thought. Now he could prove we were being harassed, intimidated, disturbed, and threatened, and not the other way around. His constant charges that the neighbors and the police were together in a "great conspiracy against me and my constitutional rights and religious freedom" were strengthened by that incident, and more so by what followed soon after.

The police took statements from Randall, Jack, Johnny, and Ron, which of course were exaggerated in the extreme to build a major case. Baker was charged with attempted murder. They also took statements from some of the other neighbors who had witnessed the event. They all disputed what Randall, Jack, and Ron had told the police. One commented, "Ron and Johnny I would describe as somewhat odd, and they're hostile toward the neighbors. I guess they're more like paranoid."

Another comment was, "I knew from the past that the Larrinagas and those others were dangerous people, and I felt Baker was entrapped. The Larrinagas have been a problem in the entire neighborhood."

One neighbor described the shooter as "very drunk at the time," and another claimed that Ron had incited Baker by calling him "pervert, drunk, and other names." He described Ron's son Randall as "like the next in command" and claimed the Larrinagas "liked to bait Baker whenever he drove by, calling him names every day."

Within a week all charges against Baker were mysteriously dropped. When he found that out, Ron really went berserk. "That *proves* a conspiracy!" he screamed, pacing up and down. "I will NOT tolerate this! They are destroying our constitutional rights!" We hurried to yes him and agree with him at every turn, so he wouldn't turn his anger on us. We were glad it was focused on Baker and the police for a change. Ron stormed to the phone and denounced everyone he could reach at the police department. "It's a conspiracy to deny us justice! We're good Christian citizens, and you're in league with those heathen neighbors of ours who are making false charges against us! Give us Barabbas and kill the Christians!" he screamed, then slammed down the phone.

Soon we had involved every imaginable authority in our dispute with our neighbors and the police department over the "conspiracy to infringe our rights." Letters had gone out not only to the police chief, but to the ACLU, the Office of the Attorney General, NBC, major newspapers, and the mayor. Within days, the police were flying over our house in helicopters, and we didn't know if they were protecting us, or doing surveillance on us. Of course we presumed it was surveillance, given the conspiracy Ron was convinced existed between them and the neighbors. I recorded, "Police helicopters went low over our house, looking down on us with binoculars." Several police cars now patrolled our remote street on a regular basis.

Amazingly, Ron still didn't run away. Nor did he stop his beatings, punishments, and general abuse of any of us during that time. In fact, his treatment of me and Jack and Philip, who had finished his stint in the service and returned home, got even worse. Ron decided that we had "failed" in our assigned tasks of writing the authorities and keeping the police at bay.

Jack got verbal lashings, more isolation, and freeze-outs. Ron didn't try physical beatings on Jack. I got the beatings, and Philip and I were deprived of sleep and food and made the victims of concentrated humiliation. Ron's heavy drinking made things much, much worse. When he was drunk, which was more and more of the time, he was mean and viciously brutal, and more sexually aggressive than ever.

On February 26, the police knocked on our door, claiming there had been another complaint about our loud radio and Ron's insults. They warned Ron, "If we get another complaint about you people, we are going to take a criminal report, and there is going to be an arrest made."

Then the neighbors got up a petition against us. They took it to a judge and got a misdemeanor warrant for Ron's arrest. On February 29, two squad cars drove up to the house. We all stood quietly in the front room as usual, peering out from behind the curtains, as Ron went out in the yard to meet them. "Mr. Larrinaga, you're under arrest," they said, and one officer quickly handcuffed him. When he saw his father being handcuffed, Randall dashed out of the house and began screaming at them as Ron had indoctrinated us to do if any authority tried to intervene in our lives.

"My father is a good Christian!" Randall hollered. "He hasn't done anything wrong, and you can't take him with you!"

Kathleen Miller ran out, too, and put her arm through Ron's, clasping her hands tightly together. "You're not taking him anywhere!" she shouted. "If you take him, you'll have to take me, too!" One of the policemen broke her grip and shoved her away from Ron. Then Janet grabbed Ron around the waist and refused to let go of him, and the cops had to break her hold on him, too. By this time all the adults and older kids were out on the lawn, and we created a big uproar.

The cops somehow got Ron away and into the back seat of the police car. They slammed the door, and Kathleen then jumped in the front seat and had to be dragged out, screaming and kicking. "You're not going to take him! He's done nothing wrong!"

Ron was hollering from the back seat, "Don't let them take me. I haven't done anything!"

Edward and Tommy ran toward the car from the other direction, and Johnny and the Millers screamed at the police.

The officers yelled, "Stay back! Stay away, or we'll arrest you, too!" Pandemonium reigned. The cops had their nightsticks in their hands by now.

"You're not going to take him away!" Johnny yelled. "Or you're going to have to take us all!"

I ran over and joined in, screaming, "No! Don't take him, don't take him!" and tried to throw myself across the trunk of the car.

"Get off the car, lady!" said a policeman, waving his nightstick. I saw another policeman hitting Edward and Tommy. Then one of the cops pulled out a canister of tear gas and started spraying it. We all started choking and gagging. We couldn't see, but we kept yelling at them.

They quickly backed the cruiser with Ron in it away, and Randall yelled, "That's my father, and we have the right to follow him!"

But the cops were already off down the hill, lights flashing and siren screaming. Johnny Spencer, Tommy, Janet, Randall, and I jumped into Ron's car and took off in a squeal of tires after the cop car. With that, the rest of the cops jumped into the other squad car and followed us. Randall could barely see to drive because his eyes were still streaming from the tear gas. At one point, even though my eyes were watering, I was leaning over the back seat and steering for him as we madly chased the first police car down the winding canyon roads. Soon we were right behind the car with Ron in it.

The other police car swung in right behind us, and soon a third cruiser pulled in from a side street and led the procession. We were going at top speed, four cars in a line, three with lights and sirens going, and we swished through the red lights along with the police cars, trying to keep up with them, sandwiched between them. We sped through the Montdale valley at top speed. We didn't know that the cops had put out a Code Three on us, believing we were armed and dangerous to them and might try some crazy move to prevent them from taking Ron to jail.

Then the loudspeaker on the squad car in front of us suddenly barked: "You in the Oldsmobile! We order you to pull over! Stop!" The two lead cars swung over to the side of the road and stopped on a wide grassy embankment right next to a high chain link fence. We swung over onto the grass, too, and stopped. The police officers came at us with guns drawn. "Get out of the car, hands over your heads!" they commanded. Terrified, we tumbled out. "On your knees! Face down!" they ordered, and pushed us roughly face down on the ground and kept us there. Then a dozen or so more squad cars, all with sirens on and lights flashing, came screaming up and pulled in around us. Their radio plea for reinforcements had been answered in a big way! We were dragged up from the ground, slammed against the fence, and searched for weapons. Then they handcuffed all of us, read us the Miranda rights, and told us we were all under arrest.

"What for?" Randall asked.

Their answer was some sort of code word that sounded like "lynching," but it meant, we learned, that we were being arrested for interfering with the process of arresting someone under a warrant. That carried a higher penalty and higher bail than a misdemeanor.

We were booked at the jail, where we could hear Ron screaming from his cell. He was lying on the floor, hollering, "I can't breathe, I'm passing out!" Then he yelled, "Help me, I'm dying!"

We immediately all began screaming again. "Help him!" Janet hollered. "You're killing him! You're going to be held responsible! He has claustrophobia, and he can't breathe!"

Johnny joined in, "Get help to him! You're killing him! He'll die if you don't help him, and it will be your fault!" We made a huge ruckus.

Finally, the boys were taken away, and Janet and I

were taken by a dark haired officer to the county's women's prison and put in a holding cell. There, we were told we'd be strip searched. I was shocked to discover what that meant. First, a heavy set woman jailer with henna red hair came and put us into separate holding cells. Mine had nothing in it but a small wooden stool in the center. "Take off all your clothes," she ordered, and left. I took my clothes off. Then two other jailers put the handcuffs back on me. My clothes were removed from the cell, and I stood there, stark naked and freezing. The matron came back in. She ordered me to open my mouth, which I did, and she looked in with a flashlight. "Raise your arms and turn slowly around." Shivering, I obeyed. "Now, lean over, grasp that stool, and spread your legs," she said. I couldn't believe I was hearing right.

"What?" I said. "You can't mean that. I haven't done anything wrong!" I protested.

"I can mean it, and I do. You're under arrest. Bend over!" she said menacingly. I turned and bent over. She unsnapped one of the handcuffs and snapped it to the stool. Then, with one hand on my shoulder to hold me still, she roughly pushed her gloved fingers inside me and twisted them this way and that, examining me vaginally. Then she did the same thing to me rectally.

At that, I choked and cried out in rage and protest. "Stop! How dare you!" It hurt badly, but also I was furious, humiliated, and embarrassed. I couldn't believe what was going on. I wanted to sink into the floor and disappear. Then I heard footsteps. The woman jailer turned around, keeping me bent over in that exposed position, with her fingers in me and spoke sharply to someone. I turned my head to see the male officer who had brought me in.

"What are you doing here? You know you're not supposed to be in here when we're doing this!" she admonished him.

He just laughed and said, "Oh, that's right, I forgot. I'll leave immediately," and he slowly walked away.

"Okay," said the matron, unfastening my handcuff from the stool. "You can put your clothes back on now." When I looked up at her, furious, she was grinning nastily at me. I was beside myself. I couldn't believe this was happening.

The matron hadn't noticed the marks and bruises I had from where I had been beaten. She was just a jailer, accustomed to treating criminals, and not a social worker. Anyway, I wouldn't have admitted to anything if she had noticed. I was far more terrified of Ron than I was of her. As I stood there, I heard the matron who was examining Janet say, "I'm making a note of your swollen legs and bruised-looking veins."

Janet answered, her voice trembling, "They're from age and my having so many kids."

We were then given blankets and transferred to a regular cell, where we were able to compare notes. Janet and I rarely had any contact with one another any more, except for punishment sessions. I knew she was angry with me about Ron, but she also realized I had no choice in the matter. However, I well knew that anything I did that was wrong or anything that I said that wouldn't be acceptable to Ron would be reported to him the minute we got out, and then I'd really get it, so I was very careful. Janet told me, "I was strip-searched, too, but the male officer didn't show up at my cell."

Jack came home from school, found out what had happened, and went immediately to a bail bondsman to bail us out. He had to put the house up as collateral, but we were all out by eleven o'clock that night. A few days later, a warrant was issued for Kathleen Miller's arrest, on the same charges they had booked us all on: "Willfully and unlawfully resisting, delaying, and obstructing a public officer in the discharge and the attempt to discharge a duty of his office."

Ron, who believed everything was ordained by some spiritual factor, decided that only one lawyer, Harold Sinkler, was ordained by God to help us. Ron gave him tons of ammunition, including all the letters we had written, all the logs of when the police had watched us, and photos of the helicopters and police cars doing surveillance. Now we had the task of barraging the world of authority with new letters. We filed suit against the police department for false arrest, brutal treatment, and the violation of regulations in the strip search of Janet and me.

Our trial was set for June. Meanwhile, we filed countersuits against the police and the city. Ron drove the attorney crazy with endless phone calls and visits, so much so that Sinkler soon complained, "Our phone conversations are endless and are terminated only by my pleading to be released from continuing. Rehashing old information over and over again is not productive." He invited Ron to "feel free to change counsel if you feel I haven't approached your case with sympathy." I was obliged to read, copy, and answer all correspondence with the attorneys and to maintain full and accurate files and logs at all times.

The case dragged on. There were several postponements. Ron was frustrated at our inability to get things resolved. We didn't know that he had decided he wanted to get out of there for a while before the cops discovered that the kids weren't in school. Meanwhile, the police had doubled their surveillance on us. They continued to use helicopters as well as squad cars. "Go to Sinkler," Ron ordered me, "and get a restraining order against the police department, to keep them from snooping around." I went to the lawyer, and he looked at me like I was a crazy woman.

"You must be kidding. No, I will *not* try to get a restraining order against the police department," he said. "I never heard of such a thing! Impossible!" I reported Harold's answer back to Ron, but that didn't satisfy him. He sent me to the library to find a copy of a restraining order, and I spent days researching the subject. Then I drew up our request for a restraining order. Ron had Johnny take me down to the courthouse to file it. Then he piled the kids in the motor home and left town, to get away from all the legal problems, leaving us behind to handle whatever came up next.

When the case for the restraining order came before the judge, I had to appear. In responding to our complaint, the police department admitted to the court that the helicopter with which they were watching us was armed. "Your honor, we are law-abiding citizens and good Christian families," I said softly, very meekly, as Ron had ordered me to do. "So, why are the police watching us with armed helicopters? Why are we being subjected to arrest and humiliating, illegal strip searches when we are only trying to live in peace as Christian families and worship God according to our conscience? Don't we have that right under the Constitution?"

The judge patiently heard me out, then told me he

could not grant my request for a restraining order against a police department, but he would see what he could do about the surveillance. I felt I had won at least that small victory to report to Ron.

When he looked over the papers, Hal Sinkler complimented me on my "legal smarts."

"I can't believe you did this by yourself, Mary, without any legal training. My compliments." It was the first compliment anyone had paid me in a long, long time, and it meant more to me than anyone could imagine. It was like a ray of sunshine suddenly beamed into the darkness of my daily life.

However, the police surveillance of us continued. In November Ron decided it was time to go to the top for help. He had me draft a letter to the President. In it, we accused the police and our neighbors of a conspiracy "to destroy us or to force us from living in peace as Bible-believing Christians." We told the President that "the mayor and the state attorney general have refused to act because of political pressure," and we accused the police captains of being "avowed atheists who have taken this vendetta upon themselves." In closing, Ron begged the President, "as the Apostle Paul appealed unto Caesar," for his help.

Soon afterward, the FBI began an investigation of the police department's surveillance of us. The investigation continued for more than a year. At the end, the Justice Department informed us they could not prosecute because there was "not sufficient evidence of a conspiracy" to bring a conviction.

Things went along like that for some time, and then the following May the police suddenly came roaring up the

hill again, and this time they arrested Jack! We were all flabbergasted. Jack and one of the neighbors, Bart Holman, had
gotten into a dispute over our fence.

"That fence is on my property," said Holman, "and I
demand you remove it!" Jack and Ron adamantly refused.
Ron started calling Holman all kinds of names, taunting him
at every opportunity.

One day, on Ron's orders, Jack confronted Holman.
"Get off our property!" Jack yelled. "You're trespassing on
our private property." Holman retaliated by threatening he'd
have Jack thrown in jail and fired from his job. Then he
stormed off and called the police. Holman claimed Jack had
shoved him and pushed him around, and he accused Jack of
assault.

We bailed Jack out immediately, but then we had more
legal papers to file and more work for Hal Sinkler, who by
then wanted Ron to find a new lawyer. However, we had an
eight million dollar lawsuit pending against the city and the
police department, so he put up with us.

As it turned out, our fence actually was inside
Holman's property line, and a few days later he came over
with a police escort and a chain saw and proceeded to cut
down our fence. There were several squad cars full of cops
on the street, and the police helicopter was hovering over-
head to keep us from interfering with the demolition.
"There!" exclaimed Holman triumphantly as the shorn fence
fell into our yard. Then they all left. We went out to look at
the pile of boards and rubble.

Ron was beside himself with fury. He made us fire off
more letters to the authorities in which we claimed "false
arrest" of Jack and "continued conspiracy" between the

neighbors and the police department. I wrote the FBI again as well as our state senator, the governor and the producers of the *20/20* television show. To the FBI I was ordered to write, "Police officers amassed in front of our home, threatening us. And they authorized and supervised the total destruction of our hundred-and-twenty-foot fence, in collusion with our neighbor, while they remained strategically placed to gun me down from a helicopter which circled the whole time, and would have done so had I come out my door to resist the destruction of our property."

The FBI never replied to that letter. At Ron's insistence, I wrote substantially the same thing to the other authorities. As the year drew to a close, we had enough legal matters pending to make anyone's head spin. Jack and I were still not allowed to speak to one another by Ron's orders. Ron was very nervous about the exposure to authorities our arrests had presented, and he almost always had a glass full of scotch in his hand. His mood swings were more unpredictable and even more brutal.

Then Ron suddenly turned on his two older sons, much the way he had on my older kids. Bobby soon broke under the terrible beatings Ron began giving him and ran away. After that, Ron raved on for days about an "ungrateful son that turns against his father." Then Ron took out his frustration on poor Randall. Randall had taken a lot of verbal abuse from his father all his life. While he had certainly been beaten by Ron on plenty of occasions, it had never been with anything like the ferocity Ron now showed in handing out punishment. Once, in despair after a particularly brutal beating, Randall tried to commit suicide, but failed. Ron punished him again, beating him unmercifully with the cat-o-nine tails belt, then isolating him from the rest of us, for "defying God's will for you in life." After that, Randall ran away, too.

"He'll be back," declared Ron confidently. "And when he comes crawling back, begging my forgiveness, I'll teach him to mock his father and rebel against God's will for him!" At that, I shivered in terror for Randall. Ron would kill him if he came back, I was sure. Randall had run away once before, a few years back, at about the time his father started punching him around for looking at Marian. But that time Randall had been a lost soul out in the world by himself, and he soon came back home. This time, though, he didn't come back. Weeks went by, then months. Furious, Ron took Randall's disappearance out on all of us. The beatings, the screaming, the blood, the isolation seemed almost beyond human endurance. But somehow we endured it, day in, day out.

Jack, meanwhile, continued working and giving Ron his paycheck. He was kept isolated from me and from the children. Though we were still legally man and wife, I'd really had nothing to do with Jack, physically or emotionally, for several years. We were both reduced to being nothing more than Ron's chattel, to do with as he pleased.

Our son Philip remained firmly in Ron's camp. Louise, Marian, and David had been banished for good from our lives by Ron for resisting his authority. Jack did little or nothing around the house and said almost nothing. He followed Ron's orders, turning his paychecks over without a murmur, never asking what was done with the money he earned. He worked around the yard on weekends and wrote letters or harangued the neighbors whenever Ron demanded it of him.

But then suddenly Jack, who unbeknownst to me was in touch with the banished children, began resisting Ron's continued demands on him and his verbal abuse and questioning of him. Uncharacteristically, he began mimicking Ron with sarcasm and saying things like, "Yassuh, yassuh, mastah, I'se hurryin'," using the old slave dialect, when Ron ordered him to do something. He started reacting angrily and violently to Ron's confrontations about how he was behaving and interacting with the "heathens" in the outside world when he went to work.

At this new and unexpected resistance from Jack, Ron backed off from abusing him, but Ron didn't give up the bullying, or the dogma. Every night during November and December, Ron would order several of the other adults and bigger children to confront Jack over on his side of the house. They'd go in a delegation and tell him what Ron had ordered them to say: "You will be eternally damned and will burn in hell for all eternity for resisting God's will for you!"

Jack now stolidly refused to listen to them, which surprised us all. "Get out and leave me alone!" he'd yell in fury. But they were determined, especially Johnny, who was very strong physically and very much determined to show Jack the right way, Ron's way.

Once, Jack and Johnny got into a nasty fight. Jack was determined to shove Johnny out of his room, and Johnny was determined that Jack would obey and sit and listen to the dogma Ron had sent him to harangue Jack with. They shoved each other hard, slamming from one wall to the other. Then Jack swung at Johnny, and Johnny swung back. As they scuffled and yelled at one another, they crashed into the closet, and the door snapped off. There was a big thud as they both fell to the floor. Johnny yelled, condemning Jack for his "wicked, evil, Satanic" behavior. My heart pounded as I heard the awful sounds of that battle, like two angry lions fighting in the jungle. If this keeps up, I thought, one of them is going to get hurt or killed. I wished Jack would listen to Johnny. He must truly be deep under the influence of Satan and that force Ron was now talking about.

Ron had read a book about something he called "jing-pa." He claimed it was an oriental practice which involved control of others to achieve your own ends. "Jack is using jing-pa to control you!" he'd storm at me. "You'll go straight to hell, because you're nothing but his chattel! He has destroyed your ability to bend to the will of God by using jing-pa!"

Even after the fight, Ron sent Johnny and the others over to Jack's side of the house to accuse him of worshiping Satan and practicing evil oriental rituals. Jack repeatedly chased them back down the hall, kicking at them, waving his fists at them. "Get out of here!" he'd shout, "I told you to leave me alone!"

He and our son Philip fought bitterly because Philip, fearful for Jack's soul, was absolutely determined to make him listen to Ron's doctrine. Philip was younger and stronger than his father, so at times he resorted to physical force. One day, Jack got so angry he yanked the doorknob off the hall door and flung it at Philip's head with all his might. It missed because Philip ducked in time, but that gave Ron the leverage he needed. He convinced us that Jack was in the grip of some evil oriental force directing him away from God's will. "He is out of control, crazy and possessed by the devil! He has tried to kill Johnny and Philip and will soon try to kill us all!" Ron exclaimed dramatically, as we gathered in the family room that night.

Unbeknownst to us, Jack had begun to emerge from Ron's spell and his iron control. With our mounting problems with the police, his own arrest, and Ron's older boys running away, Jack finally came out of the fog. He stunned us all one night by turning on Ron in a fury and ordering him out. "Out! You're through here! Get out of my house, do you hear me? OUT!" he yelled. Ron just stood there, transfixed, staring at Jack. "You, your kids, all of you! I warn you, Ron, if you're not out of my house, with your whole extended family within three days, I'm calling the police and exposing this mess to them!" That was enough to galvanize Ron into action.

The next day, Ron came to me and said, "Get yourselves packed and ready to go. We're leaving. Tomorrow. I'm not leaving you and your children in the hands of that godless man you married! He is willful and disobedient to the word of God! We can no longer stay here and tolerate his rebellious ways. He is violent and will kill us all if we don't leave."

I believed Ron that Jack had snapped and that we were truly in danger from him. I had never seen Jack display the kind of rage he had shown when he ordered Ron out. Nor had I the insight to realize how well-deserved his comments were yet. As I packed to leave, not knowing where we'd be going, for some reason the faces of the absent children swam into my mind, one after the other. Seven had gone from us: June, Louise, Philip, Marian, David, Bobby, and Randall. Only one, Philip, had ever come back. I hadn't heard from the others in years. Poor little June! Of her we'd heard absolutely nothing. I wondered how she'd fared all this time. Was she still alive? For that matter, was my Louise still alive? Was

Marian? They had simply disappeared from our lives. Now, I was terrified for Ellen and Jimmy, my two youngest children. If I didn't obey and go with Ron, I might lose them, too.

Mary Rich, age 18.

Mary Rich and Children.

"WARNING! NO TRESPASSING" signs posted by Ronald Larrinaga to ward away "the heathen" from cult home in California hills.

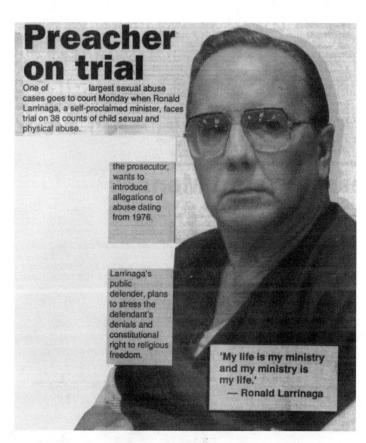

Preacher on trial

One of [ ] largest sexual abuse cases goes to court Monday when Ronald Larrinaga, a self-proclaimed minister, faces trial on 38 counts of child sexual and physical abuse.

[ ] the prosecutor, wants to introduce allegations of abuse dating from 1976.

Larrinaga's public defender, plans to stress the defendant's denials and constitutional right to religious freedom.

'My life is my ministry and my ministry is my life.'
— Ronald Larrinaga

Florida news clip: "self-proclaimed minister faces trial on 38 counts of child sexual and physical abuse."
(photo: Craig Bailey, *FLORIDA TODAY*)

Ronald Larrinaga clutches his bible at his criminal trial in Florida.

Mary, two months after her rescue.

Mary and Jim today.

7

a light dawns

Although he mouthed platitudes about saving us, Ron had a practical reason for taking us with him. He needed me on his side, in order to take the motor home. Up to then, it had never been a problem, but now with Jack in the mood he was in, Ron was taking no chances. The motor home was registered in both Jack's and my names, so as long as I was with him, Jack couldn't accuse Ron of stealing it. And he needed Philip for help and financial security because Philip could always get a job.

Everything had to be accomplished quickly, quietly, and with the utmost stealth, Ron warned us. We obeyed. The motor home was parked in the carport the boys had built into the hillside, facing out as Ron had ordered. He had craftily designed the carport so that we didn't have to pull the motor home out into the driveway in order to load it. There was a ladder mounted on one side of the concrete wall that we could climb, so we could load the vehicle through a topside port from the ladder without being seen by the neighbors, or from the house.

While Jack was at work, Ron gathered Janet, the other adults, and the children in the family room and made me take a vow that I agreed willingly to go with him. I had to repeat after him and in front of the others, "I solemnly swear that I am willing, in the sufferings of Christ, to leave my husband, my home, and all my possessions, in order to save our lives from an evil man, and not be destroyed by God for my complicity in Jack's sins against God."

By then, Ron had us completely convinced that Jack was possessed by Satan and would ultimately destroy us all, condemning our souls to eternal hell. Given that horrible thought, I was not only willing but eager to take the oath and to flee with Ron, in order to save myself and my children from certain destruction by God.

"We have no way except to flee this evil, as God has commanded me to, and go elsewhere, where we can live our lives in Christian peace in the service of God," said Ron. "Therefore, we must go quickly, tomorrow morning, without Jack knowing." He instructed us on how we would accomplish our departure. "While Jack is asleep," he told us, "you will pack and gather everything into the family room that you want to take. Kathleen will then sort through it and decide what goes and what doesn't. Johnny and Tommy will help everyone load the motor home from the ladder." We had to be especially quiet, because Jack's bedroom was on the pathway to the motor home port. We waited until one in the morning to begin loading the motor home, when we felt sure Jack was sound asleep and wouldn't awaken. The Millers watched over the younger kids and gathered up their clothes, and Kathleen sorted and packed things in duffel bags and pillowcases.

We finished loading. Jack woke up and went to work, suspecting nothing. We waited at least thirty minutes, then woke up all the kids, got them dressed, and took them one by one and put them in the motor home. I had no idea where we were going. I wasn't permitted to ask questions, or even to speak, unless I was spoken to. We pulled out, blinds drawn so no one could see into the motor home. I was ordered to lie down in the back, near Ellen. No one spoke. Everyone was drowsy by then anyway. "Stay low, make no noise, so we can slip quietly out of Los Angeles and across the California border, without being detected," Ron commanded. Johnny drove. Edward and Tommy were assigned to watch out for the police and to warn Ron if it looked like anyone was following us. By that night, we were out of California and into Arizona.

The next day, Ron ordered me to sit near him. "Over there, behind Janet," he said, "and do exactly as I tell you." His tone was cold, threatening. Then for the next five hours he grilled me. He harangued me and made me parrot back answers to every conceivable question the authorities might ask us if we were stopped. Periodically he'd pull over, and I'd be taken to the back of the motor home by him, and my bottom would be bared and I'd be beaten in front of everyone, to emphasize my abject position.

We wandered across the country for what must have been a month. Ron had plenty of cash with him from a savings account he had opened and into which, for years, he had been putting a good bit of Jack's paycheck. In addition, he had also gotten money from Philip while he was in the armed services, and some that Louise, Marian, and David sent home before they rebelled. He had also saved from whatever his own older sons had earned on construction jobs. Ron now bragged to us that he had withdrawn more than $30,000 from that savings account. "You see how God provides? God knew that we'd have to leave California one day, and He moved me to save this money, so we'd be able to leave when the time came, for God alone knows the past, the present, and the future."

"Yes, God has saved us and we must rejoice," we responded in chorus.

"Everything I do," Ron said, "is because God the Holy Spirit has told me to, or warned me, since I am the chosen servant of Jesus Christ."

It was a long month of wandering, enclosed in a small, cramped space with all those people. We were eight adults, not counting Philip, and thirteen children—twenty-one people living, day in, day out, in a narrow motor home! I know we were in Florida once, then Texas once, just from what was said. But we never stayed long anywhere, nor were we told where we were.

Ron was especially vigilant when we stopped at rest areas, and we got almost no freedom or relief from the sound of his voice, and almost no sleep. He ranted and raved at us day and night, and drank constantly. I was relieved when Philip took over the driving. Ron's fear of the police catching us heightened with each passing day, and his paranoia went beyond all bounds. He was especially vicious and brutal toward me, maybe because in those conditions there was rarely a chance for him to get me or the girls alone anywhere.

Jack's threat to inform on him had rattled Ron's composure. None of the younger kids were in school, and he was afraid the cops would find that out if we stopped too long in any one place. So we stayed constantly on the move. Finally, by March, we couldn't continue our nomadic course. Twenty-one people on the road for two months, with no new money coming in, were quickly draining Ron's financial resources. He needed to get us settled and get Philip working again earning some money for us. "We'll go to Florida," he decided, "and look for a place to live there."

"Philip," he said, "You'll need to find a job right away. We need some money coming in." Philip had been working as a satellite communications technician for a California defense contractor. He had abandoned that job on Ron's orders, to come along with us. So, as soon as we got to Florida, Philip called his boss in California. He told him there was a family emergency that required him to leave California and come to Florida, one which would keep him in Florida for a while.

He told him we were near Rock Dunes. Philip's company had responsibility for some satellite tracking sites in Florida and in other states along the east coast, so they agreed that Philip could continue to work for them, traveling to those sites to do maintenance. We were overjoyed. Naturally, Ron interpreted it to us as God's will and a sign of God's approval of our decision to leave Jack and flee California. All the lawsuits he had filed were still pending, but that seemed of little consequence to Ron any more.

"Hal Sinkler will just have to take care of them," he said. "God will show him what to do." I remembered how he had said that about my father, too, long ago, when we dumped our house on him and left for Florida the first time. But I dared not say anything.

We managed to rent a house, under Philip's name and

using his employment as credit credentials. It was way out in the countryside, in a little town pretty far south of the Space Center, on the east central coast of Florida, Palm Cay. We moved in, and life resumed its normal state. Ron beat us and berated us. Philip went to work every day, the older boys worked at odd construction jobs when they could get them, and the rest of us suffered endlessly under Ron's torment. His drinking continued unabated.

8

the real and the unreal

I stood at rigid attention at the back of the bedroom closet, facing the wall, hands behind my back, barely daring to breathe. Sweat beaded up on my body, and the tiny drops prickled as they detached themselves and went sliding down my scalp, down the sides of my nose, down between my breasts, down the inside of my legs. I had been standing there like that for hours.

The urge to move, to wipe away the drops of sweat, to turn and run was agonizing. I prayed. "Please, God, help me. Help me be obedient. Save me from more punishment."

Here and there, a faint sound told me that the household was stirring. I stole a glance sideways. The neat rows of empty clothes on their hangers seemed like watchful sentinels, waiting for me to make a wrong move so they could pounce. I held my breath, not daring to move. I felt dizzy, and feared I would fall.

I seemed to be operating in thick mists of fog that shrouded my focus and my perspective, even my ability to function. It was about eight o'clock on a Saturday morning in April, but I didn't know that. I had long ago lost track of days and hours.

Consigned to the dimness of the closet in that small suburban house in Palm Cay, Florida, I felt only cold and numbness on my bare feet and legs, heat in the rest of my body, and pain. Always pain. And hunger and thirst. Food and water were frequently withheld as punishment, and we were fed only sparingly otherwise. There were many mouths to feed, and we were always too poor, or so we were told.

Dishes clattered in the kitchen. I breathed in lightly, and the smell of coffee slid up my nostrils, bringing saliva into my mouth. Coffee! Hunger wrenched my stomach. Stealthily, I shifted one foot slightly, then the other. Sweat ran into my eyes, burning them, and the things around me blurred. Cautiously, I reached up and wiped the sweat away from my face, then brought my hand down to clasp the other hand behind my back as I had been ordered. Surely no one could have seen that one little move, that one little infraction of the rules, I told myself.

Closing my eyes, I prayed again, fervently. "Dear Lord, make me see the error of my ways. Help me to do better. Help me to be worthy enough to be back in Ron's good graces again. Help me to endure this punishment."

If I didn't falter, I might get something to eat this morning. I might not get another beating. I might even get to leave the closet. If I could just hold on long enough, just endure, Kathleen might call me to the kitchen for a bowl of cold oatmeal—a sugarless, choking paste—but welcome, oh so welcome, because with it would come a precious few minutes of freedom, a chance to sit, a brief respite from the hunger pangs gnawing at my belly.

The walls of the bedroom closet had been the boundaries of my world for weeks, maybe even a month now. When I was permitted to sleep, which wasn't often, I dropped to the floor and slept there. Ron liked it when I was banished to the closet for punishment. He would come creeping in, shut the door carefully, order me in a hoarse whisper to lie down, to take off my clothes. Then he'd amuse himself with me, away from the eyes of his wife and the other adults, away from the children's curiosity. I was his creature, totally at his mercy. He could do whatever he wanted to me.

That day, I was wearing the same light cotton dress I'd been wearing for days. Maybe I'll be forgiven today, I dared to hope. Maybe today I'll be allowed to bathe, put on clean clothes.

sometimes I fled to the closet on my own, seeking a haven. Mostly, the closet was my cell and no haven at all from the constant, unrelenting beatings or humiliation, as the pain lancing through my feet and the soreness across my back attested.

Suddenly, the door was thrown open. Ron's lieutenant Kathleen came into the closet. "These are Ron's orders," she said. She began to beat me severely on my feet and legs, using a flat piece of dried palm frond from the yard, one that was edged with sharp stickers. It made a whispering sound as she wielded it again and again, with sharp staccato slaps on my bare feet and legs.

I cried out in pain, imploring her to "Stop, oh stop! Please! Don't, ooh! I've repented and will be good." I avowed over and over again, "I'll obey, to please God and do His will." Finally, after what seemed like an eternity, she stopped. I fell in a heap on the closet floor, facing the wall, my body drawn up in a ball, trying to protect my legs, sobbing and whimpering. She added a few sharp swats across my back for good measure.

"Now get up!" she ordered roughly. "Get up and stand facing the wall!" I felt I couldn't move, but I knew that if I didn't the beating would only begin all over again. There were my blood spots on the carpet—some old, some from this morning—that grimly attested to Kathleen's diligence in carrying out Ron's commands. I pulled myself to my knees, then slowly stood on my bruised and swollen feet. Gasping, weeping, I again faced the wall, hands behind my back.

"Stand there now, and repent your sinful behavior!" She left, closing the closet door. I'd be there, I knew, until Ron decided to release me. Or punish me again.

The pain was receding somewhat, but I was close to dropping from exhaustion. Then, "Bang! Bam!" Violent banging came from somewhere near the front of the house. A searing pain ran up my leg, and I cried out, unable to suppress it. Suddenly, there was the sound of running feet in the house. The closet door opened, and some of the children quickly crawled in behind me. They were scurrying for cover. Someone was at the front door. Ron always made the children hide whenever anyone came near the house. The sound of their ragged breathing filled the closet, but none of them spoke. We stood still, all perfectly silent, as we had been taught to be. I could hear more banging at the door, louder now, and then some muffled shouts outside. It sounded like someone was shouting for Ron to open the door. I strained to hear, not daring to move, not daring to turn around. "Go out the back, go around and see who it is!" Ron's hoarse command to someone came from the safety of the hallway just outside the bedroom. I heard the back door open and slam closed. Open again, slam again. There were whispered consultations in the hall. Then another angrily hissed command from Ron, "Bring Mary here, get Mary out here!"

"Oh, God," I prayed silently. "Oh God, please, please, not me, not now." But Kathleen was already inside the closet. She grabbed my arm and yanked me around to face her.

"Get out there!" she hissed, fixing me with a glare. My heart began to pound with terror. "Ron wants you. In the living room, fast." She shoved me toward the door. I stumbled, limping, to the living room. Ron paced the room, ducking around the windows to avoid being seen from outside. He turned to me with a withering look of accusation, his dark eyes blazing in anger. My heart and stomach contracted with fear.

"It's your husband Jack and my son Randall out there. They want you."

Before I could grasp what he was saying, someone banged mightily on the front door again, shouting, "Open this door! Get this door open! We want to talk to you!" I couldn't really comprehend what was happening. I tried to focus. The pain in my feet was excruciating, I felt cold all over, and I wanted to turn and flee, to seek the warmth of the closet, to hide there with the kids. I knew from the look on Ron's face that whatever was happening, he considered it my fault, and more punishment would surely follow. Waves of fear rippled through my body and cramped my stomach. I thought I was going to faint. I didn't even notice that I had started to wet myself in terror.

Suddenly another command came. "Get out there," demanded Ron in a furious voice. "Tell them to get out of here! Away from this house!" He was crouched down, a gun in his hands, below the windows, well away from the front door. I started toward it, and he hissed, "No! Keep that door locked! Go out the back!"

Oblivious to the throbbing in my feet, spurred on by a greater fear, I stumbled out the back door, past some of the other adults and children, and ran around to the front of the house. After so long in the dark closet, I reeled from the initial impact of the bright daylight. The Florida sun had already detached itself from the horizon and glided up into the sky, coaxing a brilliant green from the ocean's depths and enfolding the day in its heavy, warm embrace. When my eyes adjusted, I saw a bunch of people in the front yard. A van had pulled right up onto the lawn, blocking the driveway. My husband Jack, whom I hadn't seen since we left California more than two months before, was there, along with Ron's oldest son Randall. Jack was pounding on the front door like a crazy man. I ran up to him past an official looking man with a salt and pepper crewcut who was standing by the van holding a walkie-talkie.

"Jack!" I screamed, "What do you think you're doing? Go away! We don't want you here!" At the sound of my voice he turned, and, seeing me, grabbed my arm.

"Mary! Thank God! I've come to get you and the kids! I'm taking you out of here. Come on! Get in the van." He was pulling me toward the van parked on the lawn. Frantically, I pulled away.

"No!" I cried. "Leave me alone! Let go of me. We're not going anywhere with you! Get out of here!" I had to get them to go away, to leave us alone, or Ron would surely beat me to death for this. "Go away!" I was sobbing, pleading with him. "Please! You must go! I don't want to go with you!"

"No!" he cried, still pulling me toward the van. "You're my wife and these are my children, and I'm going to take you back with me. You have no right to be here. That man is a madman, he has you under his spell, and I'm taking all of you out of here until you come to your senses!"

Rocking back and forth, I launched quickly into my spiel as Ron had taught me: "You have no right to my life!" I screamed. "I left of my own volition! You're the evil one, Jack! You have shown that you hate God. I left because of the fear of staying with you, because you're a devil worshiper! Get out of here, leave us alone, I *will not* go back with you! Never!"

Jack tried to reason with me. "Mary, Mary," he said more softly, "you've got to listen to me. Please. You've got to get out of here, and get the children out of his grip. Come with me, please, please."

At that, I became hysterical. Slapping wildly at him, I twisted my arm and my body, trying to escape, screaming for them all to leave. Tears ran down my face, and my heart pounded drumlike in my chest and ears. "You have to go, you have to go," I chanted. If I didn't make them leave, Ron would beat me again. I'd never get out of that closet. He'd hate me forever. God would punish me. Ron would punish me.

A barrage of angry voices shattered the morning. Johnny Spencer was already confronting Jack at the front door. "You'd better get out of here!" he yelled angrily. "We've called the cops! You'll be arrested for trespassing here!" But Jack and Randall yelled back at him, not moving. The man with the walkie-talkie just stood there, not joining the fray.

I was startled to see my son David walk up and stand next to Jack. The whole scene seemed unreal. What was David doing here? He was hollering something. It had been years since I'd seen him. He was so grown-up I almost didn't recognize him. "David?" I said hesitantly, my voice trembling. "David? What's going on?" But he didn't hear me.

The man with the walkie-talkie took a few steps toward us, as if to intervene. Through my haze of fear, I was alert to his every move. He looked official and represented some kind of threat to me, to us, of that I was certain. Then Christopher, Edward, and Tommy came to my rescue and pulled me away, shouting. Luckily, the nearest neighbors were blocks away, or they'd have the cops down on us with all the ruckus going on. Kathleen Miller had come out to join in the fray. "Get out of here. You're evil!" she screamed at Jack. "Leave Ron alone! This is religious persecution! You're trying to kill us! You're devil worshipers, and we're going to have you arrested if you don't get out of here!"

Jack had heard it all before. He ignored her and turned to me pleading again. Tears ran down his cheeks. "Please, Mary, I beg you, listen to me! Come out of this! You don't know what you're doing, or saying. Get the kids. You're going with me. Where's Ellen?"

"No! Leave me alone!" I tried to go back into the house, but the front door was locked. I wasn't about to leave with him. I knew Ron would come and get me no matter where I went, just as he had before. He always did. "Go away! Don't you understand? I don't WANT to go with you! Leave me alone!" I could feel the veins on my neck stand out as I screamed those words. I was desperate. I had to make them leave. I had been ordered by Ron to make them go. Suddenly Ron himself appeared, coming around the corner of the house from the back, Janet close behind him. Jack saw him first.

"You raped my daughter Marian!" Jack screamed at him.

"That's true!" Randall yelled at Janet. "You know it's true, Mom."

Just then a police car arrived, siren blasting, blue lights flashing. I had just raised my arms to push Jack away and noticed the bruises on my hands where Kathleen had beaten me. Quickly, I dropped them and put my hands behind me, so the cops wouldn't see the wounds. We rushed to get to the police first, before Jack and Randall, and quickly launched into the carefully orchestrated chorus Ron had taught us to use in the face of any intrusion of authority.

First we wailed, "These people are threatening us and our Christian way of life." Then we accused everyone. "They are devil worshipers, interfering with our religious life and freedom. They are trying to prevent us from worshiping God in our own home as law abiding Christians and good citizens."

Jack tried to break in. "My wife and kids are being held prisoners! Prisoners to a nut case!" The two policemen looked around. The younger blond-haired one turned and went back to the patrol car to radio for more help.

Those who had been guarding the front door had abandoned it. Everyone was out in the yard, yelling. A woman stepped out of the van and came over to talk to one of the policemen. Two little kids followed her. There was something vaguely familiar about her, but I couldn't quite place her. She said quietly to Janet, "We've come to get the children out of here," but in the thick mists clouding my brain I couldn't figure out who she was or what she wanted. The man, standing by the van in a white tee shirt and jeans, remained aloof. He kept his eyes fixed straight ahead, holding his walkie-talkie. He didn't join in the melee, which scared me even more.

"You give me back my kids!" Jack shouted furiously to Ron. "They're not staying here!"

"You get out of here. You're not taking Jimmy and Ellen!" I screamed back, terrified. I had lost my older children and hadn't seen them for years. I couldn't stand the thought of anyone taking my two youngest.

Suddenly sirens wailed, and two more patrol cars screamed to a halt in front of the house. Four uniformed policemen spilled out on the run, hands on the nightsticks strapped to their belts. "What's going on here?" demanded an older, gray-haired one, who seemed to be in charge. "Stop the yelling! Now! All of you SHUT UP!" he commanded. The other cops were pushing and pulling at everyone, separating people, trying to restore calm and establish order. "Shut UP, I said!" roared the one in charge. Most of the yelling subsided. "What's going on? Let's get the truth here, now!"

The other five policemen positioned themselves around the yard to maintain order. Ron seized the advantage and jumped in to tell his side first. "I'm glad you're here, officer," he began. "This man is threatening us with violence!" He pointed at Jack. "He has trespassed on our private property. He has torn up our yard and tried to break into our house. He dented our front door, he nearly broke it down, and he and these others were trying to force their way bodily into my home."

Jack interrupted. "I just want my wife and kids! Listen, this guy . . ."

"Shut up!" The cop silenced him. "Let me hear what this man has to say first. You'll get your chance, don't worry."

Jack reluctantly quieted. The policeman turned back to Ron.

"Now, what's the story here? What's all this about?"

"Well, this woman is his wife," said Ron, pointing to me, "and she left him, in California, of her own free will because she felt her life and that of her children was threatened. She's here with me of her own volition with her two young children. As a Christian, I felt I had to rescue her. But if she wants to go back with him, she can."

I couldn't believe what I had just heard. For the past two months, Ron had drummed into me, beaten into me, harangued into me, punished into me, my terrible mistake in marrying and living with Jack. "That evil person has delivered you into the hands of Satan," he had said. He had convinced me that to stay in God's grace I had to avoid Jack for the rest of my days. Now he was saying I could go back home with Jack? It must be some kind of test of my faith. Was Ron just testing me? That's what it had to be.

"Never!" I screamed. "I'll never go back with this evil, evil man, even if he is my husband! He is a servant of Satan. And so are those others with him. I'm staying right here!" There. Ron would surely praise me and not punish me now. I had publicly avowed my trust, my complete faith in Ron as God's chosen servant and had rejected Jack as the devil worshiper Ron had convinced me he was.

I turned to the policeman, trying to speak calmly. "Officer, I'm here of my own volition, and this man," I indicated Jack, "is trying to force me and my children to return to California with him, which I do not want to do, which we do not want to do! We are Christians, and he is threatening the will of God for our lives."

Furious, Jack shouted, "That's a lie! I let this man and his family stay with us in California, and one day when I was at work, he took my family away! When I came home, my family had vanished! I didn't know where they were. I didn't know where my kids were! I tracked them here, and it wasn't easy, believe me. This man kidnaped my family. I want my wife and my children back with me, and I didn't want the police involved, but now that you're here, I want him arrested! He's crazy and dangerous!"

"Okay, okay, now let's just hold on a minute," said the police officer. Then he said, "The lady is free to go if she wants to." He looked at me. "And where are these children?"

Ron spoke up. "Jimmy's right here." He pointed to my youngest son who had moved close to me. "And the other one is in the house, officer." He turned to Kathleen. "Bring Ellen out." Kathleen hurried around the back of the house and returned with Ellen by the hand. Both children were obviously frightened and confused by what was happening.

"What are your names?" the policeman asked them, kindly. They told him their names. "Is this your mother?" the officer asked, pointing to me.

"Yes," said Jimmy. Ellen just nodded, too shy and scared to speak out.

"And is this man your father?" he asked, pointing to Jack.

"Yes." They both nodded but only Jimmy spoke.

"Who brought you here to Florida?" the cop asked.

"Uh, well, my mother and my brother Philip, and, and, well, Ron and the family," said Jimmy.

"I see," the officer said. "Now listen to me carefully, son. Your father here claims you were kidnaped, that this man," he indicated Ron, "forced you and your mother and your sister to come with him. Is that true?"

"No, sir," said Jimmy.

Then Ellen spoke up. "We wanted to come with Mom and Philip," she said quietly. She didn't look at her father.

The officer gave Jack a look, then said to the children, "Do you want to stay here with your mother, or do you want to go back with your father?"

Ron, unable to contain himself any longer, jumped in. "I never forced them to do anything! They're here because they want to be, because they love me, and they love the Lord. We have a good Christian home here."

"Will you be quiet?" The cop was plainly irritated and, seeing that, Ron subsided. "Let them speak for themselves." He turned to the children and asked again, "Do you want to stay here with your mother, or go back with your father?"

Now Jack spoke up. "Don't you want to come back with me, back to California, back to our own house?" he pleaded.

"No, Dad, I want to stay here with Mom and Ron," said Jimmy.

"Me, too," Ellen affirmed. "I want to stay with Mom and Philip." I was shaking with relief.

Then the woman stepped forward and spoke. Her voice was quiet, but assured. "Officer, please listen to me. You need to know what is happening here. These children and this woman don't know what they are saying. They can't think for themselves, or make sensible decisions. Ron has forced my family to do things, in the name of God, that they wouldn't ever do if they were okay, but they don't really know what they are doing. It's hard to understand, I know, and it's not easy to explain how, but he has an evil hold on them. He did the same thing to me, and to his own children, and my Dad, and my brothers, to all of us here. But some of us resisted him. We opposed him and what he was doing to us, and he threw us out, me and my sister and his son Randall, banished us from our family. He did the same thing to my sister Marian. He shuts out—isolates and banishes— anyone who differs with him. He beats and abuses them. He has brainwashed my mother and everyone else in his group. They don't know what they are saying, or doing. You must help us help them. You have to get someone who knows about things like this to help us. As well as other adults, there are a lot more children in there, brainwashed like these two and my mother."

At the words "my family," my heart had leapt to my throat. Momentarily the fog lifted. The woman was Louise! My daughter! It had been so long since I'd seen her I didn't even recognize her! What was she doing here, trying to interfere? I was so shocked to realize it was Louise standing there, I didn't even try to fight her, like I did Jack. Somehow, deep inside, I instinctively wanted to avoid confrontation with her.

The cop looked doubtful but he listened closely to what Louise was saying. When she mentioned other children, he said skeptically, "There are more kids? In that little place?"

She nodded. "Yes, sir, a lot more."

The policeman turned to Ron. "Listen, are there other children in there?"

Randall jumped in. "Yeah, there sure are! Some are my other brothers and sisters, and what she just said is right. None of them knows what they're doing, what's happening to them. Only we, who have gotten out, gotten away from him, know what he's doing to them!"

The cop looked stunned. "A lot more kids? You gotta be kidding!"

Quickly, as he always did when he scented danger, Ron launched into his fervent speech. "I am God's servant, and, as God's servant, I have a fine Christian family. We all love the Lord, and the children are instrumental in allowing me to follow the Lord and do His work. We are a big family, but we love one another and work together in the Lord to do His will."

The cops now disregarded him. "Get any other kids out here," one ordered. Another banged on the front door and made Katherine Miller open it.

"Everybody out here," he called into the house. "Come out, kids." Nothing happened. The younger children were in there, all right, but they were too scared to move. In fact, they would never move unless Ron or Kathleen told them they could.

The cop in charge turned to Ron. "If there's any children in there, mister," he said sharply, "I suggest you get them out here, and fast."

"Okay, officer." Ron went up to the front door. "Come on out, kids," he called. "It's okay. You can come out."

Slowly, one by one, from the biggest to the smallest, the children filed out of the house, and stood silently.

The policemen were completely taken aback. While the others stood there as if confused, the Larrinaga children quickly went over to where Ellen and Jimmy stood. "Well, I'll be darned," said the policeman, scratching his chin and looking incredulous. "There sure were a bunch of them in there. How many bedrooms does this house have?"

"Well, there are three very large bedrooms," said Ron, nervously, "and a sitting room with several sets of bunk beds." When he saw all the frightened little kids, among them his brothers and sisters, Randall couldn't contain himself any longer.

He turned on the cops in fury. "Look, you have to do something! You have to help us! These kids are prisoners! They're being abused, beaten, and starved! Some are my brothers and sisters! He does terrible things to them! We have to get them away from him!"

"You're a liar," shouted Ron at his son. "You're a filthy liar! You're a heathen and a pervert! All you want to do is interfere with God's will in my life! You ran away from me because of your rebellion against God, and now you want to take these other children away from God and down into hell with you!"

"Shut up, all of you," the cop said, "and nobody talk until I say you can." Then he pulled out a notebook. "I want each of you to tell me your full name," he said, addressing the children. As he walked up to them, each child hesitantly gave him his or her name and age, and the policeman carefully wrote each in the notebook: Ruth, Robert, Hannah, Sheila, Dana, Luke, Mark. "Any more kids that live here in this house?" asked the cop. "If so, I want you to step up here and give me your names and ages." Amy, Edward, Tommy, and Christopher went up and gave him their names and ages. "Okay, now your two, what did you say your name was?" The cop looked at Jack.

"Jack Rich. Jimmy and Ellen are still living with Larrinaga. Except for my wife and them, the rest of us got away from him."

I had moved nearer to Ron and stood ready to back him up on anything he said. "Look, they even stole our motor home to come to Florida," Randall interjected. The cop looked at Ron, raising an eyebrow.

"That's not true. We've rented this house, and that's our motor home," responded Ron, heatedly. "I'll show you proof." He turned for the house and the cop followed him inside.

The other cops looked at each other, and one shrugged, whispering, "What do you make of this?" They seemed uncomfortable, confused by the whole situation. They didn't know who to believe, and the words "religious persecution" had an obvious effect on the officers, as Ron knew they would.

Ron and the officer reappeared. Ron was triumphantly waving the registration papers for the motor home. My name was on them, along with Jack's. "See? She brought it with us. Her name is right here as one of the owners. It's just as much her motor home as his."

"Wait a minute, officer!" Jack protested. "That's my motor home! I paid for it. She didn't! She never worked or earned any money, so how could it be hers? And I need to have it to take my family back to California!"

The cop in charge turned to the others. "I've had enough of this family's squabbles. Okay, okay, now you listen to me, all of you. I'm not going to decide anything right now.

The motor home, the woman, and the kids can all stay right here for the moment. They're here of their own free will, and said so. But you others say they're not. Well, we'll look into all this and decide about the motor home later. Now, I think it's time you people go back in your house," he looked at Ron and me, "and y'all," turning to Jack, Randall, and Louise, "leave here and go on about your business. And don't bother them, you hear? The lady says she's here of her own free will, and she obviously wants to stay, and the kids want to stay with her." They started walking to their cars.

"No, wait!" Ron suddenly spoke up, and the head policeman stopped and turned to him. "I want this man arrested!" Ron demanded, pointing at Jack. "I want all of them arrested! I don't want you to leave without arresting them! They're trespassing, threatening us! They intend to harm us! That's why we left California and came here, to get away from them. That man is abusive." He again pointed to Jack. "And my son is a liar and a crazy heathen."

"Okay, okay," said the cop, wearily. "Enough. I'm not arresting anyone right now. I've told them to leave and not to bother you, and they better do what I say. We'll come back later with a complaint form, and you can fill it out and sign it. But we're not going to arrest anyone right now. Now y'all clear out of here, hear?" The man with the walkie-talkie still hadn't moved from where he'd been standing the whole time. Louise went over and joined him, and they left in the van. I still wondered who he was, and I still felt threatened, some-how, by him. A minute later, Jack, Randall and David pulled away in their car. Then the cops got in their car and left, too.

9

abandonment

We all hurried inside. It was hot, and the tiny living room was barely big enough to contain us all, but we all crowded in and gathered around Ron, who was sitting on the couch with his fists clenched, Janet next to him, Kathleen next to her. I was fearful, but his anger had, for the moment, been drawn to Randall and Jack and everything that had just happened. "God will punish them, you'll see," he cried. "They are filthy liars and heathens and under the influence of Satan. But God will win, and we will do God's will for us." At that we all yessed him and confirmed his righteous indignation at all that had transpired. It still nagged me, in the back of my mind, that he had told the cops I was welcome to go with Jack. Was he abandoning me? Or just testing my faith?

Ron sent the younger children to the back rooms to play. "You watch them," he told Katherine Miller. "No one is to go outside today." Katherine hurried away to watch the children. Ron got up and began to pace nervously around the room. He stopped only to lift the curtain slightly and peer out into the front yard. "It isn't over," he said, as if to himself. We all stood quietly, saying nothing. "They'll be back," he added, again to no one in particular. "Once they start, they never leave you alone. Now that they know we have a lot of children here and how many bedrooms, they'll come back and make trouble. I gotta get out of here!" He turned to Janet and Kathleen. "We have to go. Now. Right away." They jumped up without hesitation. "Okay, everybody, hurry! Into the truck and the car." Kathleen went for the children. Ron turned to me, with a wild sort of look in his eyes that struck fear into me. "Mary, you're to stay here and face them. You'll know what to do. The first thing you must do, you must do," he repeated, riveting me with those eyes, "is swear out that complaint and get Jack arrested. You're his wife, so it's up to you. You have to protect us, you're the only one who can do it. They won't listen to me. I'll be back for you soon, and you better be able to tell me he's in jail." I shuddered looking at his face. "If they ask where we are, say that I feared for the children's safety, because of the threats of Jack and Randall. Tell them the rest of us left because we wanted to avoid inevitable violence to the children."

"B-b-but," I stammered, daring to speak, "what about Ellen and Jimmy? Are you taking them, too?" Fear clogged my throat.

"No, Ellen and Jimmy can stay here with you. And Philip will be home in a couple of days. They can all help you. Tell Philip I'll call him. But I have to go now. It's too dangerous. We've gotta get out of here now!"

Within the hour, they were packed and gone. Just like that. I stood there, alone with Ellen and Jimmy, dazed. I knew it was now my job to stand at the front lines, to keep Ron and the rest of them safe, to keep him out of the hands of the police, and stop anyone from going after them. I had new responsibilities, a new mission. Suddenly I found new strength. At last I was worthy again. He had named me his defender, his lieutenant. I was proud that he felt he could put his trust in me. Again and again, I went to the window. Lifting the curtain, I peered out, guardedly, watching for the cops to return. I jumped back when lightning suddenly flashed, followed by a deafening crash of thunder. It was starting to rain.

I didn't know it, but Jack, Randall, and David had not left. They'd only pulled around to a side road and waited for the cops to go. They knew Ron's habits and had figured he'd probably run. They were hoping to catch us, to show the police Ron lied about what he claimed to be. They figured they had some time, so they'd gone to a drive-in nearby for a cool drink. As their van and car were moving slowly through the driving rain back toward our house, the truck and station wagon carrying Ron and his family roared past them, both vehicles headed northward. Randall wheeled the car around, tires screaming, and set out in hot pursuit, chasing them north in blinding rain at speeds of up to a hundred miles an hour. They had no way of knowing that Ron had left me, Ellen, and Jimmy back at the house in Palm Cay.

As they came up beside Ron's station wagon on the interstate, Edward bumped their car, and they slid off the embankment on one side and were so shaken up they gave up the chase. Louise and Jack, meanwhile, had driven the van to the police station in Palm Cay. They found the same two cops and told them Ron was trying to flee and that Randall and

David were giving chase. The police put out an all points bulletin to other stations in northern Maynard County about the two vehicles Ron was driving, extending it to other counties as time went by, but they were too late. Somehow, Ron managed to give them all the slip and was soon out of Florida. Where he was heading, no one knew.

Back at the house, unaware of all that was taking place, I posted Jimmy to watch at the bedroom window, so I could cover the side windows with sheets. I told Ellen to sit quietly and warn us if she saw or heard anything. I was anxious to remember everything, as I should, for when Ron returned, I would have to report to him in detail as he always required us to do, and I would not be punished for forgetting anything. I picked up the wall phone in the kitchen, to see if it was working. It wasn't. Randall had cut the lines.

I felt a sense of panic at that. "What if Jack comes back and I need to call the police again?" I murmured.

"Maybe I can fix it, Mom," Jimmy offered. "Maybe I can just twist the lines back together and it will work." I was so driven by fear and urgency, I almost let him try it. But then reason took over.

"It's much too dangerous for you to touch those wires. You could be electrocuted." Suddenly I remembered the short wave band radio Ron always listened to. We didn't know how to work it, but we fiddled with the dials for a while, trying to get a signal to come in. After an hour or so, with no success, we gave up on it. "I'll have to go to a neighbor to call the phone company," I said hesitantly. But I was afraid even to do that. Going to a neighbor was always looked upon by Ron as a transgression. We were never supposed to get involved with our neighbors. Ron was the only one allowed to talk to them, and he was usually shouting at them and condemning them as heathens, especially if he'd been drinking. And he'd been drinking, more and more in the past couple of years.

Now, I was in a real dilemma. "I have to get help," I said under my breath. But how? I had no transportation. I walked slowly to the nearest neighbor, who lived several blocks away.

"May I use your phone, please?" I asked when she answered the door. "Ours seems to be out of order, and I need to call the repair service."

The gray-haired, petite woman seemed reluctant at first, but then relented and let me come in. "Okay," she said, pointing to the phone. Somehow, I convinced the telephone repair service that this was an emergency, that we needed the phone reconnected immediately. They promised to have a man out to our house before five that evening. Relieved, I retraced my steps, having evaded the neighbor's curiosity about who I was and where we lived.

"Oh, just down the road a ways," I told her. "We're new and don't know many people yet. We'll be fine, thanks."

A few hours later, a repairman came and fixed the phone wires. I felt a great sense of relief. Now Ron could call us, and I could call the police if Jack and Randall came back. Still, when Ron got back, he might hit me anyway. I went looking for the belt Ron always used to beat me and the children. I knew I needed to hide it so no one would find it. But it was gone. Kathleen must have taken it, or hidden it.

Late that afternoon, two policemen showed up with a complaint form. "I'm Sergeant Seeley," the dark haired officer said, "and this is Officer Taylor. Now, where's that guy and the rest of the kids?" He looked around. "Where is every-body?"

"They left," I said.

"Oh? Where'd they go?" he said, surprised.

"I don't know, he didn't say. They just left. Ron said he feared for the children's safety. They were afraid my hus-band and the rest of them would come back."

"I see. And he left you here by yourself, with your kids?"

"Yes," I answered, "but that's just temporary, until things settle down. Then he's coming back for us."

Officer Seeley didn't say anything, and he had a poker face. I worried that he wasn't believing my story. I elaborat-ed, giving him a long tale of woe about how abusive and dan-gerous Jack was. I insisted on filling out a complaint.

"I want you to arrest my husband, and not let him, or those others be free to harm us," I said.

"Well, ma'am, I can only take your written complaint and turn it in for processing. Why don't you just write down there exactly why you feel your husband should be arrest-ed?"

Then the sergeant went out to his car and came back with a woman in her forties with short brown hair streaked with gray. She was carrying a briefcase. That surprised me, because he hadn't mentioned anything about any woman with him. I felt a prickle of alarm. The woman took out a piece of paper. "I'm Clare Hartman from the Department of Health and Rehabilitative Services," she said, showing me her credentials, "and I'm here to check on the children. It's a routine thing, something we do whenever there's a complaint like this." At my frightened look, she continued, "There's nothing to worry about. I just want to talk to them for a few minutes." She turned to Ellen and Jimmy. "Are you all right?" she asked. They nodded. She smiled, trying to convey warmth but only half succeeded. "I need to take you both in another room and ask a few questions without your mother there. Is that all right with you?" she asked them. They looked at me questioningly, and I nodded, feeling numb. They went with her.

The two policemen stayed with me. I continued complaining to them about Jack, but I kept one eye on the door to the back room where the woman had taken the children. A feeling of nameless dread had overtaken me. It was tightening my chest and making it difficult for me to breathe or think. I didn't need to think, however, to reel off my litany of complaints about Jack to the policeman. Ron had drummed them into me until it was like reciting a speech learned in school.

Clare Hartman came back into the room; Ellen and Jimmy followed her. "Mrs. Rich, I'm going to take Ellen and Jimmy with me for tonight. I think, for their welfare, they need to be away from here for a while."

"What? What's wrong? Why are you taking them?"

"We feel it's best for now." Then, seeing my anguish, she said kindly, "Don't worry, they'll be back tomorrow." I was not consoled by that, but I knew somehow that I mustn't show my fear or concern, even though I wanted to scream and shout and keep her from taking my children, but I kept my emotions tightly under control.

"Okay, if you're sure they'll be back here in the morning, and if the police say they have to go." I looked at the sergeant, and he nodded. "Okay, then, but I don't like this. I don't like my children being taken from their Christian home to stay God knows where or with what kinds of people," I said, trying to convince them that I was a good mother, and we had a good home with Ron, with nothing to hide.

"They'll be fine," Clare Hartman assured me.

The kids were obviously scared, but they didn't say anything. Mrs. Hartman opened the front door, the police escorted her and the children to her car, and they all left. I peeped out watching the tail lights of their cars disappear into the growing darkness. I felt scared, and very alone. I began to cry. What was happening? More tears fell, then I made myself stop. Ron was depending on me to handle things, and I had to keep my head together. Despite my resolve, I didn't know what to do to get things back on track. I needed to think. I went into the kitchen and sat at the table. Hunger knifed through me. I jumped up and rummaged in the refrigerator, grabbing an almost empty jar of peanut butter and spreading it on a couple of hard pieces of bread. Gnawing quickly at my sandwich, fearful that Ron would walk in at any moment and find me stealing food, I mentally renewed everything I'd done and how I'd handled myself, to be sure I had done whatever Ron would have expected me to do. I knew he would hold me accountable for every action and every word, every expression on my face, and I feared I might have done something wrong, or missed doing something he thought I should have. Most of all, I dreaded him finding out they had taken the children away for the night. I was already thinking of how I'd handle my next encounter with Ron, how I'd protect myself from his certain wrath. Never were the children allowed to be alone with other adults. Never. And here the authorities had my two, and I had let them take them. Thirsty, I went back to the refrigerator and took out a milk carton. Pouring some milk into a glass, I quickly drank it down. I sponged all evidence of my meal from the table. Ron would be furious to know the kids were away. But what could I do? I couldn't keep two policemen and a social worker at bay all by myself. I went to the living room and cried some more.

Then I heard noise out front. I jumped to the window and peered out into the twilight. Randall and Jack and David were back, with the police. They banged at the front door. I opened it a crack. Randall said, "Ron has skipped out and is leaving Florida."

"I don't believe you!" I shouted.

"Mary, come with us," he begged me. "Come out of this, now."

All I could think of was that Ron had left Florida. Ron had abandoned me. "They're going to keep the kids," Randall added.

"No!" I screamed. "My children will be back tomorrow. The woman said they would. And I'm not going with you. Not now, not ever!" I resolutely closed the door in their faces and locked it. I heard them drive away. I thought, Ron has left Florida. I wandered slowly through the empty rooms, savoring the silence, the solitude, the relief from fear, the first I'd known in years.

Even with all that was happening, there it was, deep in the back of my mind, a feeling of relief in knowing that with Ron and Kathleen gone, I wouldn't be put in the closet, I wouldn't be beaten. Not tonight, anyway. I needed time, time to think what this meant. Time to plan what to do. But right then I was weary, so very weary. I was too tired to think any more, or care what anyone did. I looked at the clock in the kitchen. It was only nine o'clock. Numb, I fell onto the single bed in the front bedroom, the one we always used as a lookout point to see who might be approaching the house, and soon fell into exhausted sleep.

The next day dawned hot and humid, with thick cumulus clouds scudding across the sky. I was up bright and early and fixed myself some cereal, feeling sinful and guilty, and ate every bite. Then I sat down and waited for something to happen, but the morning moved on and there was no sign of the children, or of Ron. There was no sign of anyone, for that matter. The house and the street were eerily silent. I lifted the curtain and cautiously peeked out. I don't know what I expected to see. The fronds of the single palm tree out front drifted lazily back and forth in the sultry breeze. A bird scurried across the lawn, in search of a tidbit. The motor home was parked in the driveway as the police had ordered. After all the turmoil and uproar of the previous day, I found it difficult to cope with all this silence, the absence of any activity. I prowled through the empty rooms, then returned to the living room and paced, watching the phone, willing it to ring. The hours crawled by. Around noon, the phone suddenly shrilled, and I jumped in fright. I raced to answer it. It was Clare Hartman, the woman from HRS. "We're going to keep your children a while longer, Mrs. Rich," she informed me.

My heart fell. "Why?"

"Just for observation," she said brightly. "No need to worry. We need to check a few things out. Please come to the HRS office on Pine Street on Monday at ten o'clock, Mrs. Rich. We want you and Mr. Rich to be here to answer some questions, and we'll make some decisions about Ellen and

Jimmy then." I hung up, thinking of her words. "We'll make some decisions," she had said. I knew from her tone that I was not included in that "we" who would be making decisions about the children, and that really frightened me. I was also fearful because she'd said that Jack would be there, too. That meant that they had ignored my complaint and hadn't arrested him. Ron would be furious at me for that. He had specifically ordered me to see to it that Jack was arrested.

I paced up and down, back and forth, all day long, not knowing what to do. I couldn't drive the motor home because the police had ordered us not to move it, so I had no transportation, and worse, no money. Where could I go, anyway? I didn't know where the children were, or what was going to happen to them, or to me. Pine Street, she had said. I didn't even know where that was! Rage rose in me. How could they do this to me? I hated Jack, and I hated Ron, too, but I needed him. Ron would know how to get us out of this. It would be worth the beating I'd surely get for letting them take my kids, for not getting Jack and the others arrested, if only he'd call. He'd be able to help me. Ron always knew how to handle cops, how to get them to go away and stop bothering us. I prayed for his call, but the phone remained silent.

Things were beginning to get out of control, and I didn't know how to handle them anymore. I was terrified they'd call the authorities in California and find out about the mess we'd had with the police department and the FBI there. I was still in a fog, but not so deeply that I didn't recognize the danger signs all around me.

Whenever the truth of my situation tried to force itself to the surface of my consciousness, I pushed it back down, deeper and deeper, completely denying it. I denied it with words, with lies, with actions, with every weapon available to me. I denied it to the point that I believed only what Ron had taught me to believe. I spoke only those lies he had taught me to speak. I was terrified to be with him, more terrified to be without him. I was terrified of God, and of what God might do to me if I challenged Ron Larrinaga, whom I believed, with all my heart and soul, was truly God's chosen servant.

There was no road back. In fact, I didn't know consciously that Sunday as I went through my first day alone in years that I needed a road back. I was still too deeply involved to realize what had happened to me, to all of us. Even the words that Jack had screamed at Ron: "You raped my daughter Marian," though they imbedded themselves in my brain like tiny blowdarts, did not jolt me enough to bring me back to reality.

At that time, Philip was still totally under Ron's influence, and, like me, completely devoted to him and his doctrine. When the police came back to the house at Palm Cay that first day, Jimmy had placed a call to Philip in Hilton Head, South Carolina, which is where he was working that week, and he put Philip on the phone with one of the police officers. The officer asked Philip about his father Jack Rich, and if he knew anything about what Randall and his Dad had charged Ron with regarding his sister Marian. Philip told the officer, "My father is a violent man and tried several times to kill me in California. He is trying to take his wife and children back, and they don't want to go with him." When the officer pressed Philip about his sister Marian, he admitted she was his sister but said, "Marian Rich left our home more than six years ago, and since that time we've had no contact whatsoever with her. She's lying! Marian is a loose girl, living as a tramp." Which is what Ron had hammered into us all, over and over again, about Marian and Louise.

Philip and I were the last two still firmly under Ron's spell. We were totally convinced, totally under his domination, and no one could tell us otherwise. We totally believed at this point that Jack was evil, that Louise and Marian were tramps, and that Randall was a wicked fallen son trying to incriminate a righteous father, who was a chosen servant of the Lord. When Philip received the phone call from Jimmy about the weekend's events in Palm Cay, he made the decision to take time off and to hurry back to Florida, to help me preserve our Christian family.

Jimmy, in that confrontation over the phone, seemed already to have changed somewhat. He even got angry when Philip said he would come to the HRS hearing but would refuse to help Jack and Randall about what would be done with him and Ellen.

That Monday Philip and I went together to the hearing at the HRS office. It was an informal session, but I was uptight and in knots. Bob and Louise had gone. It was Jack, Randall, and David against Philip and me. Jack spoke first, saying that as their father he wanted custody of Ellen and Jimmy, and that he'd like to take them back to his home with him, "away from my wife and this man Larrinaga. They are abusing them and keeping them out of school. I am employed and own a home. I can feed them, clothe them, and see to it that they are not mistreated and that they are placed back in school, properly, which their mother can't and won't do."

I spoke up. "My children are very well taken care of,"

I retorted hotly, "and they are clothed and fed properly. They are not in school yet because I just moved to Florida, and I'm not yet settled properly, but I have every intention of getting them enrolled as soon as possible," I lied. Then I turned to Philip. "My son Philip here has a job and is perfectly capable of supporting us until I can find a job." Philip nodded yes at that. "I left my husband in California because he was violent, because he tried to kill my son Philip on several occasions, and I never want to go back to him, nor do I want my children to be given to his custody. He will harm them."

Philip, ignoring Jack's glare, added, "He withheld his paycheck from his wife and left them with no money, no food, and no home."

That was another lie, but we would have said anything to keep Jack from getting Ellen and Jimmy. Jack, outraged, jumped up and started to scream at Philip, "That's a rotten lie, and you know it! You're sick!" The social worker quieted him, and he sat back down. The Department of Health and Rehabilitative Services then announced their decision.

"We are not giving either parent custody of these children," an official said. "We have reason to believe there is substance to charges against both parties. Therefore, until we have examined the case further, the state will retain custody of Ellen and Jimmy. They will be sent to a detention camp for the time being."

I was shocked and horrified. They were taking my children away from me! I felt a deep pang of loss and desolation, and then fear overwhelmed me. How would I ever explain the decision to Ron? He'd beat me unmercifully when he found out. Jack turned and gave me a look so full of hatred and despair I flinched. "I hope you're happy, Mary, with what you've done to us and our family," he said bitterly. "Haven't we all suffered enough? Now with your stubborn will and your lies, you've lost our kids!"

I refused to speak, or even look at him. Something in my heart stirred for a moment, some glint of realization of what I'd done, but I pushed it back down. Then, on our way out, Randall turned on Philip in fury. "You miserable rat! You still believe that sonuvabitch my father, don't you?" he accused. "Now your brother and sister are gone, like the rest of us had to go: June and Ronnie and me, and David and Marian and Louise. Now Ellen and Jimmy, too, all because of you and that miserable, no-good father of mine! He's sick! Don't you understand? Crazy! And so are you! You're brain-dead, man. You're all brain dead! You need to wake up!" And, with those words echoing in the air, Randall stormed away down the hall. But what he had said was filed away in my brain, to be chewed over later.

Neither he nor we could leave. The HRS officials told us to wait out in the hall until they dismissed us. We sat on separate benches, not speaking. An hour later, they came out and said that Philip and I should go and get the children's clothes from the house and bring them back to them, and that Jack, Randall, and David were free to go. They left about ten minutes ahead of us. When Philip and I got to the house, the motor home, which in the midst of all these events the police had allowed Jack to reclaim, was parked in the driveway. Randall and David had broken into the house and were busy searching it.

Enraged, Philip jumped out of our car, ran to the motor home, and grabbed the keys out of the ignition. Randall saw Philip take the keys, and he dashed from the house. "Philip, give them back," he demanded.

"I will not!" hollered Philip. "You've broken into our house and are stealing our things! I'm calling the police. You're thieves!" With that, Randall lunged at him, and Philip punched Randall in the mouth. They both fell to the ground, fighting, and David ran to join in. I took that opportunity to race into the house and call the police. Soon two squad cars came screaming up, with three police officers and one plain-clothes detective.

"They've broken into our house and are stealing things!" I cried. "Hurry! They have a whole bunch of our stuff in the motor home."

"We're not stealing anything, officer," David said. "We're just taking what is rightfully ours. These are my things, and they stole them from us when they left California." The officers searched the motor home and returned some of the items found in there to us, then took Randall and David away in the squad cars, but later released them.

Jack was with them when they came back to get the motor home. Philip had pulled the battery wires off so they couldn't take it. "You're not going anywhere with this until we have the police search it again. I know there's more of our stuff in there!" he said defiantly. At that, Jack got so mad he went for Philip and chased him back into the house. While they scuffled, Randall and David hastily reconnected the wires to the battery.

"Stop that! You're nothing but thieves! You're taking our things. Leave us alone. You're children of Satan!" I was jumping up and down, crying and screaming, trying to kick them and pull them away from the motor home, but they got it started. Jack came out, shoved me aside from blocking the door to the motor home, and they took off. I ran into the house and called the cops again.

Philip jumped into his car and roared off in pursuit of his father. The weary police arrived. I sent them after them, too. The police pulled both Jack and Philip over. They searched the motor home again, but came up with nothing, so they let them go. That night, Ron called. "File a police report accusing them of grand theft," he ordered Philip. "You must list that they took things of enough value to get them arrested and thrown in jail." He dictated a list which Philip dutifully copied down. The next day, Philip filed a police report accusing Jack, Randall, and David of grand theft, of stealing more than $4000 of items from us, including a camera and a gun, items which Ron actually had in his own possession.

That night Ron called again. "Leave Ellen and Jimmy there in Florida with the HRS, and you and Mary can come and join me," he told Philip. But he didn't say where he was.

I got on the phone, pleading, "I can't leave my children without knowing what's happening to them."

"You are disobeying the will of God for you, and you will be punished for that!" he said angrily, furious at me for refusing to obey him. I trembled, but stood my ground against him for the first time in many years.

The next morning, Philip and I attended a formal court hearing about Ellen and Jimmy. I thought we'd be able to present our case to the judge, and we were prepared to be very convincing—Ron had taught us well—but when we got there we were only asked to fill out papers and make written statements. Jack had apparently been there earlier, filled out his papers and made his statements.

In our statements, Philip and I accused Jack of abuse and violence against me and the children, and we said it was he who had kept the children out of school in California, not me. We said that Philip's income would be enough to support me and the children if they'd give us custody of them, and then we signed the papers. A blond-haired woman from HRS told us, "Another court date will be set in the near future. Meanwhile, Ellen and Jimmy will continue to live at the detention home."

Jack and the others left that afternoon for California. We learned that he'd visited Ellen and Jimmy at the home on their way out of there. I was so upset about not having the children, I didn't know what to do to get them back. I was also in terror that at any minute Ron would come back. He called again that night and told us to call the School Board in California and report Jack to them. "Speak to the Superintendent of Schools only," he said, "no one else." We immediately called, and somehow Philip got the Superintendent on the phone.

"My father Jack Rich attacked us. He's a very violent man. He was arrested in California and was on probation for assaulting a neighbor." He told the Superintendent that Jack had lied to the HRS, trying to gain custody of his children, and said it was Jack who had kept the children out of school all the time we were in California. The Superintendent was very nice to Philip and expressed concern about Ellen and Jimmy. He assured Philip he would speak to Jack and deal with the matter. I breathed a sigh of relief when Philip hung up.

"Jack won't have a job, or an income, for long. Then he can't hope to get custody of the kids," I said. It didn't occur to us that Jack might have gone to the school authorities before leaving California, and explained everything to them, and told them why he was leaving for Florida.

Ron called us again that night and praised us for filing the theft report and calling the Superintendent. "Leave the kids and go to Atlanta, Georgia," he ordered Philip. "Look for work there. That way, you'll have money to fight the custody and be out of reach of the Florida officials." He asked to speak to me.

For the first time in years, I discounted his words. I told him, very firmly, "I'm not leaving Palm Cay, and I'm not going with Philip to Atlanta, or anywhere else, until I get Ellen and Jimmy back. I love you, Ron, and always will, and I respect you, but I can't abandon my children." I was braver now, knowing he was in another state and couldn't bring immediate punishment down on me. I had no intention of deserting Ellen and Jimmy. He then asked to talk to Philip again, and that gave me a cold chill. I wondered if he was going to order Philip to beat me into submission.

But Ron told Philip only that I was a rebellious and incorrigible woman. That Philip had no choice but to abandon me, to leave me to whatever God's will was for me, and for him to rejoin Ron. I listened in fear as Philip, obedient to Ron's every whim, agreed to give up the house at Palm Cay, leave me there, and meet Ron at a place called Slidell. I didn't know where Slidell was. Ron told Philip to give me some money and have the realtor give the deposit back to me. He said to buy me a week's worth of groceries before leaving. Ron said I could also have whatever of the furniture or household goods I wanted.

I didn't try to dissuade Philip from going. I even

helped him pack up the car and the U-Haul he rented. At half-past seven the next morning there was a knock on the door. I opened it to find a policeman standing there. My heart was in my throat, but all he wanted was for Philip to sign the affidavit of grand theft against Jack, Randall, and David. Philip signed, the policeman left, and shortly afterward, Philip pulled out of the driveway. I watched his car disappear down the road, and I stood there alone in the front yard of the house that was no longer mine, wondering what would happen to me, and what would happen to Ellen and Jimmy, now. I had a $100 to my name, and no job, no home, no transportation.

10

chains and freedom

I was completely alone for the first time since I was nine-teen. I cleared out the house, got the deposit back from the realtor, and began to look for a job.Slowly, painfully, hesitantly, I tried to think on my own again. However, my mind was still heavily buried in the fog Ron had created.

My first job was as temporary companion to an elderly lady not far from where we had lived. It put a roof over my head and food in my mouth for a few weeks, but soon it was over. I got another temporary job at a printing company that would only last a few weeks, the owner warned me, but it allowed me to lease a tiny apartment in Palm Cay, closer to town.

For transportation I had only an old bicycle, which Philip had left for me, so I had to bike the several miles back and forth to work every day. Having a car wouldn't have helped, since I had no money for gas. The bicycle, too, was a whole new experience for me. I could barely make it back and forth to work, sometimes in driving rain, and I was physically spent when I arrived home at night, too tired to even think. During the first two weeks, I just threw myself down on the bunk bed Philip had left me and cried myself to sleep. I didn't have a phone because I couldn't afford the connection fee.

Moreover, I had little money for food. After I paid the deposit on the apartment and the first month's rent, I had only sixty-three cents left to last until my first paycheck, which wouldn't come for two weeks. I survived by going to a government surplus food place and getting cheese and rice, and by doing a little of the hated "bygering" I had learned from Ron. I tried to get food stamps, but was disqualified because my name was still on the motor home and the house in California. Desperate, I went to HRS and begged them to help me. They made a temporary exception for me until I could file for support from Jack, and allowed me food stamps of about twenty-five dollars a month, but even that small amount was a life saver to me.

All too soon my job at the printing company ended, and I was job hunting again. It was a struggle but I had managed to survive a full month on my own. As I lay in my bed those nights, with no one yammering at me or punishing me, I finally began to think, and to question. Was it right that we had to be beaten and punished so terribly o he point of fearing for our lives in order to follow the will of God? Was I really that bad a person that I needed to suffer so to submit my life to God? And what about rape? God certainly wouldn't condone Ron for raping me, or my daughters, as a method of getting us to follow His will. And why did Ron tell me one thing and mean another? Despite these periods of returning rationality, I missed him and still feared him. He had been the dictator and conductor of my daily life for years. Every day, I expected to return home and find him standing there, ready to bring retribution for my rebellion down on my head and body.

Though I felt anxious and worried, my new freedom, however perilous, was a great joy to me. Then on a summer day a new terror entered my life. The state's attorney's office ordered me to appear for interrogation and to give them a sworn statement. That sent fear racing through me. I was told that if I did not appear as ordered, I would be arrested and charged with child abuse. I didn't know who I was more afraid of, Ron or the HRS. As I stepped out of my apartment to go and testify, a bolt of lightning streaked down, and there was a great crash of thunder. I jumped in fright. If God were going to strike me dead, as Ron had threatened He would if I ever made a statement to the authorities, now was His chance. I was truly amazed when, at the end of the day, after making my sworn statement to the authorities, I was still alive.

They asked me a lot of questions about Ron and our relationship with him and his treatment of the children. I was still enough under Ron's spell to vehemently deny everything. I even denied that he had mistreated or abused any of us, or that I had mistreated my children. I again blamed everything on Jack, as Ron had instructed me to do, accusing him of being an abusive father. I again demanded that my children be returned to me. However, the HRS, finding "probable cause" that the children had been abused, decided to keep them pending further investigation and adjudication by the courts.

I was devastated at that but had to keep trying to put

my own life back together again in order to fight for my children. The miles of biking back and forth to work, on top of the many injuries I'd received at Ron's hands, were taking a heavy toll on my physical health. I hurt everywhere, it seemed, but especially in my back, my neck, and my legs. I had no money to seek medical help. But I discovered that the apartment complex had a pool area with a Jacuzzi, and every night after work I went directly there and slid gratefully into the hot whirlpool to soothe my frazzled body and nerves. I didn't care that it was as hot outside as it was in the Jacuzzi. I was just grateful for this one small respite in my day and for the comfort it gave me.

One night I was joined there by another woman, who introduced herself as Olivia Ramirez. "I am from Puerto Rico," she said. "Where are you from?"

"Oh, here and there," I said, "but I was born in California and lived most of my life there." Slowly, tentatively, we became acquaintances, then friends. After a while, I opened up to Olivia and told her part of my story. She had become my first friend in many years. She had a car and offered to drive me to my meetings with the HRS and to the grocery store. Once she took me to visit the children in Orlando, since I had no other way to get there to see them. That was a red letter day for me, but Ellen and Jimmy were unhappy at the detention home, and I was horrified at what I felt were un-Christian conditions there.

Olivia also introduced me to the local Sharing Center, a place where people down on their luck or in trouble could go to get practical help. There I found I could get a whole grocery sack of used clothes for only a dollar! And a bagful of canned food for a dollar, too! That was a gift from God, I felt, because I desperately needed clothes for work and couldn't afford to buy any.

A few weeks later, Jack flew in again for the court hearing on the children. When he saw me, he asked me again to return with him. "You have to come back, Mary, and we'll pick up our lives again, for the children's sake, if nothing else. Please listen to me. I know Ron has your head all screwed up, but after a while it will be okay again. I think that if we tell the court we're going to make a home again for the children, away from the Larrinagas and the others, they might give us custody of Ellen and Jimmy again." He begged and pleaded with me, tears in his eyes.

I looked at the man who was my husband, standing there outside the courthouse, begging me to return to him, and suddenly a wave of understanding swept over me. I felt compassion for him and gratitude that he had still wanted to rescue me and even now was willing to take me back, but I realized I could never go back. Not to him, not to that house, not to Ron Larrinaga, not to all the horrible memories of the past years. "Jack," I said quietly, my heart pounding with fright as though it would break, "I can't go back with you. I'm still pretty confused. I have to stay here and rebuild my life and put this behind me. Can you understand? All we've suffered has made a future life together impossible. I won't return to Ron, but I will try to get custody of the children, and then maybe we can talk again. But I don't think I can ever come back to you. And certainly not now. I am too mixed up about myself right now. I don't know what God wants me to do. You have to leave me alone and let me work this out."

"You?" he said. And then Jack, who had suffered with me so long, exploded. "You're confused! What about me?

What about our kids? Who was it got us mixed up with Ron? Who was it who had to follow him everywhere? You're at fault, too, Mary! Just don't forget that! And you're my wife, and you belong with me and our children. You've made a mess of all our lives, but you won't face it." He stormed away, furious at me again, and left. Both of us lost. The state of Florida again decided to retain custody of Jimmy and Ellen.

A few weeks later, through HRS, Jack sent me money from an income tax refund, asking them to please convince me to buy a car with the money, so I could give up the bike and would be able to visit the children more often. I was working part-time at a fabric counter at the new Wal-Mart, but I was looking for a full time job that would sustain me. I was sure that was all I needed to get my children back. When I got the check and Jack's instruction to buy a car with it, I at first rejected the idea. I was terrified at the thought of driving again. I didn't even have a license anymore. Ron only allowed me out when he, or one of the boys, drove me. But my friend Olivia and the HRS lady convinced me I should get a car so I could be independent and wouldn't have to bike to work in the rain. I started studying for my driving test.

A couple of weeks later, Olivia drove me to my test, and, miraculously, I passed it. Then she took me shopping for cars. I finally decided on an old beat up Mercury that seemed in decent mechanical shape. To me it was wonderful. I drove it straight from the used car lot to Orlando to see the children, a distance of seventy miles each way! For the first time, I was allowed to take them off the grounds of Great Oak Village, and we went to a local ice cream place for lunch and ordered sundaes as dessert, to celebrate. The children were thin, but looked tanned and reasonably happy. And this made me feel grateful.

In June, Jack wrote asking me to come to California to discuss our situation. He sent me a round trip ticket. I decided to go, because I wanted to see the other children and my own family again, if they would let me. Petrified, since it was my first time on an airplane, I flew out there and was terribly airsick all the way. I was reunited with my daughter Marian, and I saw Randall and David again, too. "Can't you come to your senses and realize who Ron is, and what he has done to all of us?" Marian cried to me.

But I still had my fears and doubts, though I was beginning more and more to question Ron and his motives in my mind. David was very cool to me and almost turned away from me. He still hadn't forgiven me for the whole scene when they came to rescue us, and he, rightfully I know, blamed me for everything, all that had happened to him and the others, and especially for Ellen and Jimmy's present predicament.

During that visit, I was also finally reunited with my father and brothers, whom I hadn't seen in so many years. But during those terrible years in Tartola I had lost my mother. And my only sister, still smarting over what she considered my callous behavior in refusing to visit my mother as she lay dying, wanted nothing to do with me. And no wonder. Now, as I tried to reestablish some ties with my father and brothers, as I poured out my story to them and expressed my regret, I still couldn't believe I'd never be able to see my mother again, or talk to her. That realization was a terrible blow to me.

Dad was glad to see me again. However, seeing him a

prematurely feeble man, aged by my mother's untimely death and grief over my life, was also a shock. Our reunion was a tearful one, and I vowed then and there I would never be forced to lose touch with my father or my brothers again. I hoped some day I'd be able to reconcile with my sister, that she'd find it in her heart to forgive me about Mom, that somehow she'd come to understand.

Jack and I met for coffee in a quiet place in Tartola. I felt I had at last come to terms with my feelings for him. I looked at him, and my heart lurched with pain for all we had been through together. I still wasn't fully out of the spell Ron had cast, but had become my own person enough that guilt was starting to surge to the fore and almost overwhelm me. "I can't come back to you, Jack, ever," I said softly. "Too much has happened. We can never make each other happy again. I want a divorce. My brother has agreed to help me with the legal filing."

Jack picked up his coffee cup and took a sip, then put it down again before replying. I gazed at him in surprise. I hadn't noticed anything different initially, but now I did. Jack looked better than I had seen him look in years. He had filled out, and his look was one of quiet self-confidence. He was a man who looked content, almost happy in fact. "Well, Mare, I was willing to do anything to give our marriage another try, for you and for the kids. But if you won't then I will accept your answer. I hope that by now you've gotten over any idea of letting Ron back into your life, or near Ellen and Jimmy, or you'll never get them back."

I shook my head wearily, still somewhat unsure that Ron wouldn't return and take control of my life again, so I said nothing, just toyed with my coffee cup. It slipped by me that Jack had said "you'll" not "I'll" or "we'll."

"I'll get the kids back, I won't stop until I do," I said with more confidence than I felt. "And when I do, I'm going to make a home for them myself." Jack fidgeted for a minute or so, then, clearing his throat nervously, he suddenly smiled shyly at me. It was like seeing a rainbow break through the clouds. He was quite handsome when he smiled. When had he become so handsome and self-assured?

"Well, Mare, if you're sure of what you are saying, I won't fight you on a divorce. I have to get on with my life, too, you know. Neither of us is getting any younger. I've met a young lady, a nice lady, with whom I think I can make a new life and be happy. I hope the same will happen for you some day, Mary, when you finally come around to facing what Ron Larrinaga really is, and what he has done to us and our kids. God knows it's a wonder either of us can feel anything for anyone, ever again. You and I have not been husband and wife for a long time now, and I guess you're right about not trying to get back together again. I promise I'll help you financially, and I'll help you in any way I can with the kids." I truly wished Jack happiness and, though we could never be husband and wife again, we parted as friends.

My father insisted on flying back to Florida with me to check out that I was okay. "Besides, I want to see the grandchildren I've missed." He spent a week with me, and we visited the children in Orlando. Dad cried when he saw Ellen. "She looks like your mother," he said softly. "She looks like Mom." We were able to get them out for the Fourth of July weekend, and we all took Grandpa to Daytona Beach. He walked and splashed in the surf with Jimmy and built sand castles with Ellen. Tears came to my eyes as I sat

on the beach under the umbrella that shaded me from the hot
July sky, watching them. These younger ones had not experienced family life, ever. The air smelled fresh and clean, and
the soft sound of the surf falling rhythmically against the
shore soothed me. Suddenly I had the first glimmer of realization of how awful our life under Ron's influence had been,
how much we had all missed and suffered because of him.
My mother's face flashed before me, and a terrible grief
welled up in me, but I desperately pushed it back down. Way
down. I couldn't break now. There was too much at stake.
And I'm glad now that I held to my sanity, for that would be
our last visit with Dad. He died soon after he returned to
California. I was glad that he saw us that one last time as
happy, almost normal people again.

My brother helped me through the legal maze of getting my divorce from Jack, and I landed a full time job working in food service at the local hospital. I spent weekends driving over to Orlando to be with the kids. The Sharing Center
remained a welcome lifeline for me, and I budgeted carefully so I'd have money for a treat for the children on weekends.
I had heard nothing from Philip and nothing from Ron, and
none of us had any idea where they were, though Randall had
told me when I was in California that he was still working on
finding them. Randall was still determined to rescue his
younger brothers and sisters and bring his father to justice.
After my father died, I no longer pretended to myself, and I
let some of the deep grief I felt come to the surface. But I still
feared Ron and feared he'd return and take over my life
again, as he had so many times before. I remembered how he
had come back after years apart and moved back in with us
again. I went through my days automatically, marking time,

waiting, but for what I wasn't sure anymore.

In the evenings, after work, I'd meet Olivia at the pool or the Jacuzzi, and we'd talk and relax. Life was looking a little better every month, and I was growing emotionally and had gained some confidence in myself again, though that was still a problem for me. I had felt for so long that I was nothing and no one, unattractive and unworthy, as Ron had hammered into me so often. Even Jack had found someone he liked more than me. For the first time, I felt self-pity. I felt used and abandoned, and sorry for myself. I had spent my life mistakenly thinking I was pleasing God and had not only suffered terribly for my fanatical beliefs, but had finally lost everything and everyone I loved.

After a few months, I realized I couldn't keep up my heavy schedule seven days a week, with weekends traveling back and forth to Orlando. I decided to look for a job and a place to live nearer to the kids. Finally I found a job and moved there. The kids were happy to have me living nearby, where we had a home to go to on weekends instead of an ice cream store. Things were better, but I knew I couldn't keep floating from menial job to menial job. I needed a skill that would give me more permanent employment prospects.

I had been awarded a small monthly allowance in the divorce, so I was more financially secure than I had been before. Jack was also sending the courts child support for the two children. My father, God bless him, had left me enough money to take a training course of some kind. I had again become interested in clothes and makeup and how I looked. I decided to go to beauty school to train to be an esthetician and become licensed to do facials and skin care.

However, though I was taking steps toward a more

positive future, my present life was still difficult. The court had ordered me to undergo medical tests and to begin psychological counseling before they would consider awarding custody of the children to me. Most of my external injuries at Ron's hands were healing, for they were mainly bruises and abrasions, except for a shin injury from being repeatedly kicked, but I had to have a hysterectomy. My memory and brain functions seemed impaired, too. I had been slapped and hit in the head so much and been under such constant terror and stress that I couldn't do complex tasks or follow a sequence of commands. Loud unexpected noises made me freeze in terror.

More than a year had passed. Ron and his extended family and my oldest son Philip seemed to have simply disappeared, dropped from sight, though Randall still had a detective looking for his father.

I now began extensive deprogramming in the form of psychological counseling. My recovery proceeded in fits and starts as I made a few steps forward and then slipped back again a step. Nevertheless, I was progressing. And, in the back of my mind, I knew I would have to one day soon do something to stop Ron from doing more harm, but how would I find the strength? I missed Philip. In fact, despite all that had occurred, I missed *all* of them terribly at times. Moreover, I wanted Philip to get away from Ron's influence and have a chance to have a normal life again, too. How was he, I wondered, and what was happening to Janet, the others, and the Larrinaga kids? They were my family, too. I cried often. I was still so mixed up. I didn't want to think about the past: it was too painful to deal with. So, as that summer ended, I tried to put it all out of my head and concentrate on rebuilding my life and getting my younger children back.

Meanwhile, Philip was with Ron and his family in Slidell, Mississippi. Ron was busy telling him what a blessing he was to him and was pleased that Philip had brought some furniture and stuff with him. Ron didn't know where they were going and was very paranoid and upset that Ellen and Jimmy were in custody, and that the law had begun looking into the family's life.

Ron was still drinking heavily and was even more reactionary and violent with all of them than he had been before. Ron told Philip that I was an evil woman, comparing me to Lot's daughters. He said I didn't care about Philip, and that I would even cost Philip his job. Some people in Philip's company told him that they had called him in Florida and that I just told them that he was gone and I didn't know where, which was true, but Ron used that as an example of how little I cared about Philip.

With me gone, Ron turned on Janet more than ever. They had a brutal confrontation at one point, because Janet didn't want to continue wandering around. She wanted a house, and she demanded that they find a place and settle down. She wanted Ron to go to Haverland, Texas, where she knew some people, and find a home there.

Ron finally gave in to Janet, and they and the others settled in Haverland. Philip got a job there. At first, they all lived in an apartment for about three months, but then they bought a house on Las Brizas Avenue. They started attending the local Baptist church, where they had a church school, and Ron allowed the younger kids to go to school for the first time. Ron was very fearful of the authorities at that point, so he didn't dare keep the children out of school the way he usually did. The older boys had to find work right away. Ron's sons did a lot of odd jobs, billing themselves as the "Christian Brothers Construction Company," but Philip was the main wage earner.

As Philip said later: "Ron almost always had a glass in his hand when he harangued us, or punished us at this point. I should say here that physical beatings, though severe, were only a small part of the torment Ron unrelentingly poured onto us. The emotional and mental abuse we suffered, the dreadful blows to our self-worth and self-esteem, inflicted far worse damage than the physical beatings did. He worked continuously, slowly, insidiously, over a long period of time to break down our free will and to create total doubt within us that we were worthy. Before long, he'd destroyed all will to rebel against his harsh physical punishment and all ability to think or reason for ourselves aside from what he told us to think, or to do. It's hard for anyone who hasn't been in that situation to understand it, I know, but what happens is you lose all ability to reason or act on your own. You follow this person because he is your source of ability, of motivation, of capability to act.

"At times, Ron would try to increase or expand the 'flock' under his control. Once in California he tried to bring another family, a Jewish family, into our circle, but they broke away just in time. There was another family in Texas, too, a retired military officer and his wife, and he nearly succeeded in moving us all in with them, which was his usual way of establishing territorial domination over others, but then the officer got wise to him, I guess, and distanced himself from Ron. And from time to time, he'd tell me about families he'd moved in with in Pennsylvania and Florida, during his missionary trials, but when he began his faultfinding and haranguing, they usually ended up throwing him out, and then he'd come running back to us.

"It wasn't long after we'd moved into the house in Haverland that the neighbors began to realize that something bizarre was going on there. We boys—by then we were men in our twenties, but Ron's treatment made us boys mentally and emotionally—did a lot of work outside, in the yard and around the house. Ron would come out, drink in hand, and harangue us with sermons in a loud voice. He'd go on for hours on end, more because he wanted the neighbors to hear it than for our benefit. We'd heard it all hundreds of times before. Sometimes he made us line up at the curb and stand at attention to listen. Naturally, the neighbors noticed this strange behavior. Pretty soon they started to get annoyed at his shouting, and then they started complaining. "Shut up!" they'd yell. "We want some peace and quiet around here!" Of course, that just made Ron madder at the "heathens and perverts," and he stepped up his outdoor sermons and began hollering back at them, like he had in California, and calling them names.

"Ron was still beating us all pretty horribly, but he always kept the windows closed and music playing loudly when he did it, so we were pretty sure the neighbors couldn't hear what was happening. Sheila and Christopher, particularly, suffered abysmally at Ron's hands during that time in Texas. Sheila was beaten nearly every day when she came home from school, for some supposed infraction of Ron's rigid rules about mixing with the heathen. I remember in particular one occasion when Ron was after Christopher, who was running from him, and Ron finally caught him and threw him down on the floor and was punching him and beating him with his fists, and Tommy jumped in. Just then, Ron aimed a really major kick at Christopher, but caught Tommy in the stomach instead and sent him flying, the wind knocked out of him. Tommy just lay there, gasping, trying to get his breath back, and Ron was momentarily distracted by that, so he let Christopher go.

"Ron was paranoid about the authorities in Florida finding us, so we weren't allowed to make contact with Mom or anyone. Now and then I wondered how she was doing, and what had happened to my brother and sister, but Ron had me completely convinced they were evil, and condemned to burn in hell for disobeying God's will for them, and I should not allow myself to be drawn into their evil circle."

In late summer I got a phone call from Ron's son Randall, telling me that the detective had traced Ron and Philip to several different states, including Oregon, but hadn't yet located him. "I have mixed feelings," I said slowly. "Can you understand that?"

"Of course I can," Randall said. "We're on his trail, though," he bravely assured me, "and we'll find him." By then I'd decided once Ron had been found I was going to have to take a stand against him, but I was fearful of doing it, fearful that he'd still find a way to punish me. It's hard to explain that kind of deep-seated fear and dread, but it still exerted some control of me, despite the progress I had made.

A few weeks later, Randall called again. He sounded jubilant. "Mary! We found them! We found Ron and Philip! They're in Haverland, Texas." Hearing his words, dread filled me.

"Randall, I know I have to file criminal charges against your father with the state's attorney's office. I know we have to try to save your brothers and sisters and to get Philip away from him. It's going to be so hard and I'm still so scared."

"My father is nuts, don't you understand?" Randall broke in. "Crazy nuts! Someone is going to get killed one of these days if we don't do something to stop him."

I stood there, gripped by fear and terror again. I knew I had to be the one. Randall had been gone too long, and California wouldn't touch it. Florida was our only hope. Ron had done enough to me and all the kids there to file charges against him and make them stick: he would go to jail for what he did. I had to do it for the kids. For Marian. For Randall's sisters and June. How could I leave those other kids with him? "I know what's right, Randall," I told him, "but I need a little time to think."

After I hung up, I sat and stared into space. Then I started to cry. I wasn't ready for this, not at all. I was progressing with my psychological counseling, and I knew now, in my heart and mind, that what Ron had done and what he had brought us to was terrible and very, very wrong. I also knew that I had some blame. That was the hardest thing to accept, that I bore a lot of responsibility to my own kids for what had happened to them at Ron's hands. I was already sick with guilt and worry, exhausted mentally and emotionally. I was still beleaguered with the paperwork and red tape of fighting the HRS officials, and measuring up to the demands of the family court judge, so that I could regain custody of Ellen and Jimmy. I felt overwhelmed and sorry for myself. I cried off and on for two days. My heart was pounding with fear. My mind was weary. My kids were shut away from me.

I knew from bitter experience that Ron's violence had only increased over the years. Not that he had ever not been abusive. But I realized now that the more he drank, and the more he abused us, the worse he got. Now, without me to turn on in anger, I knew that the children, Janet and the others, and Philip, too, would be suffering the brunt of that unfettered rage and brutality. Ron might beat one of them badly enough to kill them. Or get out a gun and shoot them all. I knew he was capable of doing it.

Was it fear, or was it loyalty to Ron that held me back? Fear of what he might do to me? Did I still believe he was the "chosen servant of Christ" and that God would punish me if I denounced him to the police? I examined my heart and my conscience, and for the first time really faced what kind of monster the man was. Finally faced that I had been completely wrong about him. He wasn't speaking for God, or for Christ: they would never behave, never speak in that way.

Having been distanced from Ron and his influence for more than eighteen months by then, I was finally, painfully, and slowly coming out of the mists that clouded my ability to reason, to think for myself. I was beginning to realize, and come to terms with, the real truth about Ron Larrinaga. Even so, I had only begun what was to be a long hard road toward freedom.

No, I reasoned, what was now holding me back wasn't my fear, but concern for my two children. I didn't want to start anything that might jeopardize my chances of getting Ellen and Jimmy back, anything that might complicate our lives, upset the delicate balance of sanity and rapport we had tentatively achieved. I was finally moving my life, and theirs, in a positive direction. They were in school, and both were doing very well in their studies. I was doing well at my job and with my counseling. I was working with the social workers and the court-appointed advocate for the children. I felt I was nearing the point where they might be with me for longer periods than just weekends. The mere thought of dealing with Ron Larrinaga, and all that might entail, sent chills running through me, and made me physically ill.

For the next few days and nights I paced my little duplex apartment, up and down, up and down, thinking. Memories of the horrors we endured were suddenly being unlocked and crowding my brain. Pictures of the children suffering his brutality flashed through my mind almost nonstop. I could see Ron clearly, glass of whiskey in one hand, a belt in the other, shouting at Edward and Tommy, beating them unmercifully. I could feel his hands on me, feel the shame and revulsion. Ellen, crying in a corner. Marian, her eyes filled with fear. Louise, shut up in a closet day after day. Beatings, endless beatings. Kathleen's hand raised, with the belt cut in strips, hitting me, hitting me. Blood on the walls, on the floor, Kathleen herself terribly beaten by Ron. Crying aloud in horror, I forcibly blanked those terrible images from my mind and ran for the safety of my room and my solitary bed. But sleep didn't come. At night I tossed and turned, unable to shut out the memories, unable to stem the onrushing tide of guilt and grief that overwhelmed me. I cried until I was wrung out, exhausted.

One by one, behind my tightly closed eyelids, the Larrinaga children's faces would slide past: Mark, Luke, Christopher, Dana, Edward, Tommy, Ruth, Sheila, Hannah, and little June, the sad-eyed child of long ago. They seemed to be looking at me with reproach. "How could you abandon us? How can you, now that you know the real truth, leave us in his clutches? Save us, you must save us. You. You. You."

I shivered, pulling the blankets around me, and thought again of my own children. That Philip was still with Ron frightened me. Poor Philip! Ron had even forced him at times to beat me, his own mother. "Oh God," I cried aloud, "please help me, please give me a sign of what I should do! I'm so tired, so confused . . ." But God had already given me a sign, I knew. He had sent those children to march relentlessly, hour after hour, through my consciousness.

The next morning, resolutely, I picked up the phone and dialed the number of the state's attorney's office in Titusville. "This is Mary Rich," I said slowly. Taking a deep breath, I went on to pronounce the most formidable, frightening words I had ever uttered: "I've decided to file a formal complaint against Ron Larrinaga." The woman I spoke to made an appointment for me to be there at 4:30.

Perhaps I expected too much, but when I arrived at the office after the agonizing forty-five minute drive over there, I was told, "I'm sorry, ma'am, but the state attorney has left for the day." I couldn't believe it. I had decided to file charges, had made an appointment, had driven all the way over there, and no one had bothered to stay? I stood there for a moment, stunned, and then the emotional dam broke and tears poured in a deluge. I laid my head down on the counter and just sobbed, completely startling the receptionist.

"You don't understand," I cried angrily. "That man is crazy! I had an appointment! He's going to hurt those children, maybe kill them! We have to do something." I was gasping words and phrases out incoherently. "I said I was coming, why didn't they wait? He held us all hostage, all those years. He beat us, nearly killed me, raped me, raped my daughter," I babbled. The poor receptionist tried her best to calm me. She gave me a tissue, patted my shoulder, then led me to a chair.

"Just sit over here for a minute, please, and try to calm yourself, okay? I'm sorry about your appointment. I'll go see if there's anyone still here who can talk to you. Just wait over there." I collapsed into the chair she indicated, still sobbing uncontrollably. She went for help and returned with the Assistant State Attorney, Sally Anderson. She took me into her office, and there I poured out, between sobs, as much of the real story about us and our lives with Ron Larrinaga as I could.

The tale Sally Anderson was hearing for the first time was one so bizarre, so unbelievable, that she just stared at me. "You have to do something. He's probably killing his own children now, in Texas," I pleaded, when I finished. She had been taking notes while I was talking, but I knew from the look of horror and disbelief on her face that she probably didn't believe a thing I was telling her. She thought I was a nut case who had somehow wandered in. I couldn't really blame her. No one in their right mind would believe the story I'd just told. The sad thing was that it was all true.

"Thank you for coming, Mrs. Rich. We'll look into this immediately and get right back to you on it," she said sympathetically. Then she quickly ushered me out. She was just placating me, I thought furiously. She wanted to get me out of there so she could go home. I was overwhelmed with grief and frustration and beyond all reason. My dealings with the court system during the past year had shown me that nothing gets done quickly in those tangled state bureaucracies.

"You have to hurry and do something right away!" I cried desperately as I left. "We just found him again, and if we don't do something now, he'll leave and run away, and we can't afford to hunt for him again." But I was already out the door, and she had turned back to her office.

Well, I tried, I consoled myself on the long drive back to Orlando. At least I could tell Randall that I tried. I didn't believe anything would be done by the state attorney, but I was wrong. Once Anderson checked the files on the children, she immediately opened a criminal investigation. For the next several months, I stayed in touch with the state's attorney's office, urging them on. Randall also barraged Sally Anderson with calls from California, begging her to believe what I had told her and to do something and do it quickly, before worse things happened to the children. He had sent the detective to Texas to keep Ron under surveillance. The detective was interviewing Ron's neighbors, gathering all the evidence he could to help Sally. To us, the process seemed glacially slow, but they were making progress, they assured us. They had received information of suspected abuse from California, and were methodically, tediously, tracing Ron's activities.

"Look, you two have to understand something. We can't rush in and arrest him on your say so, even if we believe everything you and his son say," Sally old me. "We have to be certain we have enough strong evidence to make the case prosecutable. That takes time. You'll just have to be patient."

Meanwhile, the guardian appointed by the court informed me she was preparing papers to present to the judge that she hoped would help me get permanent custody of the children. "When do you think that will be?" I asked her anxiously.

"Soon, I hope," she promised with a smile. "Probably sometime early next year."

But events in Texas had already taken a turn that would bring everything to a head before the New Year dawned.

On November 10, I got a call from Sally Anderson. She sounded excited. "Mary," she said, "there have been some developments in Texas on the Larrinaga case that I think you should know about. Texas HRS moved in and has removed the five youngest children into state custody."

"When? What happened?"

"I don't know. I wish I could tell you more, but we have no details. I'm telling you everything I know. I'm sure you're anxious, and I'll call you as soon as I know anything more. I want you to be ready to fly there—you, Ellen, and Jimmy—to testify at the custody hearing on what you've told me. I'll be back in touch with you soon."

I hung up in a state of shock. The Larrinaga kids, like Ellen, in state custody. How had it all happened? "Please, God, let us not be too late to save them all." Frantically, I dialed Randall's number in California, but there was no answer. The phone just rang and rang.

11

texas debacle

I stayed by the phone, waiting for word from someone, anyone. It wasn't long in coming. "Be ready to leave day after tomorrow," Sally informed me. "Ellen and Jimmy will go with us." The next thing I knew I was on a plane, headed for Haverland, Texas. For a woman who had never flown anywhere in her life and was terrified of airplanes, I was suddenly becoming quite the cross-country air traveler! This time, though, I couldn't give in to my own fears, because I couldn't show Ellen and Jimmy I was afraid. They were terrified at the thought of being near Ron again and needed all the reassurance I could give them. Which wasn't easy, since I was terrified myself. We'd all have to face our fears in the days to come, I realized, as Sally briefed me on what I'd need to do.

When we arrived in Haverland, we were met by a man from the prosecuting attorney's office and taken to a hotel downtown, not far from the modern, semicircular stone court house. Sally went to their DA's office to fill them in on the charges I had filed in Florida, and they said they would work to amend the charges at the custody hearing, based on this new information.

We had no sooner settled into our hotel than the phone rang. It was Randall. "Randall!" I cried, "Oh, God, I'm so glad to hear from you! I tried and tried to call you. Where are you? Where's David? What's happening?"

"I'm right here in Haverland. David's here, too. We've been here for nearly two weeks. That's why you couldn't reach us. We've been helping the detective maintain surveillance over them, so Ron won't get away again," Randall told me.

Jimmy immediately left to go meet Randall and David, and then he decided he'd stay with one of the neighbors on the cul-de-sac where Ron was living, so he could help keep an eye on the Larrinaga house. Jimmy hated Ron now. He and Ellen were ready, they told me, to testify, and so were Randall and David and Marian and the others.

Randall told me Marian was expecting a baby soon and couldn't come, but they were trying to contact Louise to testify. Jack had refused to come. "He said he couldn't afford to take any more time from work," Randall said annoyed.

"That doesn't really surprise me," I said. "It's probably true that he can't afford to take time off. He took so much time off to try to rescue us and again during the early months of the custody hearings on our own two children."

I doubted that Louise would be able to come, either. Louise and Bob were both stationed in Germany, and I doubted they would let her come that far to testify. "I notified Louise," Sally told me. "She's trying to get home on leave so she can testify. That is, if Bob can manage the kids while she's here." I crossed my fingers. Louise would be a big help to us, if she could just come. Then I felt guilty and awful about the way I'd treated her when she tried to rescue us.

The hearing began November 14. The next morning, I picked up a San Antonio newspaper. There it was, in bold headlines: "REPORTS OF CULT BLOODY BEATINGS EMERGE IN COURT." The story recounted Randall's comments about how it had been to live with Ron. Seeing those things in front of me in print made me feel sick and faint. My heart pounded in fright. For a long moment I wanted to run away with Jimmy and Ellen, back to safety in Florida. How could I walk into a courtroom and face Ron? But I knew I had to go on. I took a deep breath and tried to calm my fears and deal with reality. Horrible as it was, it couldn't be allowed to continue. The man was a monster. I knew that I needed to come through for them and not fail the children.

Within days, the trial began. I stood outside the courthouse when Ron and Janet and the older kids arrived to testify. Philip was there, and Amy and Edward and Timothy and Ruth. Seeing Ron in person again, my heart began pounding but it was not as damaging to me as I had feared it might be. Maybe because we were outside, in strange surroundings, and in a crowd. There were television reporters and newspaper reporters everywhere, demanding interviews of all of us, and Sally Anderson stayed close beside me.

Ron allowed no visible reaction to show on his face when he first caught sight of me in front of the courthouse. In fact, he behaved as though he didn't see me at all. Inside the courtroom, he didn't look surprised, either, and I had to wonder if he knew me. I looked so much different from my former self that even the Larrinaga children barely recognized me. I had cut my waist-length hair short and dyed it a light brown and had put on some weight, so I was no longer just skin and bones. I was learning facial care and makeup techniques in my esthetician courses, so I was wearing make-up. I had new clothes and earrings. I looked like a regular person, and that was surely strange to Ron. It was quite a startling transformation from how I had looked when we lived in Palm Cay and in Tartola.

After the first lurch of adrenaline at seeing Ron again—a quick, painful clutch of terror at my heart—he became nothing more than the abusive monster he was, someone who had taken over my life and my children's lives and the others, including his own children.

I was distressed to see my son Philip remain firmly in Ron's camp, even after, one by one, we took the stand and told the truth about all the terrible things Ron had done to us, to all his extended family, especially the children. But I understood, after my sessions with the psychologist, how mind control works, and why Philip was behaving the way he was. Louise had arrived from Germany as we'd hoped, and she tried to talk to Philip in the hallway of the courthouse, but he'd quickly walk away when she approached him, waving her away as though to ward off something evil.

"He brutalized the children, he raped me, he beat me, he will be brought to justice," I proclaimed to the television reporters as I left the courthouse that day. I felt good about myself for the first time. I was suddenly liberated and able to speak out at will.

I knew that every night back at the house Ron probably pounded into them how we were wrong and he was right, and we were an abomination against God, and gave them no opportunity to think otherwise. Even so, down deep, I had hoped that maybe after Philip heard me testify under oath about how Ron had raped me and saw his sisters again and heard their testimony, he would react and come over to our side. But he seemed more determined than ever to stick up for Ron, and later he testified strongly in Ron's behalf.

Philip said later: "During the custody trial, every night, Ron harangued us for hours, going over what had been said, consulting his Bible, directing us as to how our testimony should be. As I sat there in court during the custody hearings, I was still totally under Ron's influence, and even more so now that he had lifted the isolation and brought me back into the fold and into favor. As each person testified, I watched Ron carefully. If any of what they were saying was true in the eyes of God, I reasoned, Ron would twitch, or show signs of nervousness, or guilt. They had sworn on the Bible, after all, on God's holy word. Even Ron wouldn't dare defy that, or God would strike him dead, as he had told us so many times would happen to us.

"I knew with my rational mind that the others were telling the truth about what happened, and I had seen or experienced most of it, but I was still mentally and emotionally immature, brainwashed, and in total denial. On a couple of occasions, I must admit, my boat was severely rocked, especially when my mother, and then my sister Louise and the younger girls, said under oath that Ron had raped them and sexually abused them. That was the most shocking thing I could have heard, and if I had believed them for even one second, I probably would have gone after Ron and beaten him senseless then and there.

"But Ron didn't act at all nervous, he didn't twitch, he

didn't even blink when my mother said what she did. He just continued reading his Bible, as though they were talking about someone else, not him.

"So that convinced me beyond any doubt that it was Ron who was acting in the name of God, and my mother and the others were all liars, and lewd and lascivious people, as Ron said they were. He even answered my concerns about the young girls being molested. He convinced us in his nightly tirades that the people at the jail and in the schools were abusing the young girls in their custody and then blaming their own sexual acts with the girls on him. 'My daughters are virgin Christian girls,' he told us, 'being exploited by heathens!' Seeing him so calm and self-assured, I was fully for him, and eager to testify in his behalf, and convince everyone that this man of God, this chosen servant, had done nothing wrong. All these people claiming he abused them were evil, and defying God's will."

As the trial went on, Randall testified. "We never had a happy childhood," he said. "My father used the Bible to create a hell that we lived in every day. We never went to school, never had friends, never did normal things. He was a devil, a demon, a crazy man." Asked why he had decided to try to prosecute his father, he said, "The sexual molestation of my sisters was the last straw. He does that to them, and tells them it's okay, it's his way of showing God's affection to them. He tells them they must not question him because God speaks through him as His servant. He uses his power over the kids to alter their minds and control their behavior. He's a cult leader, and he's not a minister, no matter what he says. He's a self-appointed minister. It's a Jim Jones (the cult leader

whose followers committed mass suicide in Guyana) situation. Before I got away, if my father had ordered me to kill
someone, I would have. You need to understand how mind
control works. It's just so insane."

Ron's response, too, both inside and outside court,
was predictable. "It's all a conspiracy," he said. "It's lies, lies
by those who want to destroy a good Christian family. We are
not a cult, we're a family. It will all be revealed, by Jesus
Christ. My son is a hippie, and on drugs, and lives in promis-
cuity. He is lying about our life, trying to destroy our family.
I am a man of peace, of Christian love."

As I watched them, and myself on the newscasts on
television that night, I could see that it would be difficult for
an ordinary person to decide who was lying and who was
telling the truth. Ron Larrinaga and his supporters looked
very plausible and spoke sincerely. So did we. "I give him
credit for one thing," I remarked to Sally. "Ron trained us all
very well in how to speak up convincingly."

On Thursday, November 17, the three youngest
Larrinaga girls managed to escape from state custody. The
judge was furious and demanded they be found and returned
at once. Ron's lawyer, claiming the girls said they had been
abused in state custody, had them stay with some of his
friends in Haverland, refusing to turn them over to the state.
I'm sure Ron grabbed that opportunity to reinforce his power
over them and to exhort them to admit to nothing. The judge
requested that they be voluntarily returned. Ron's lawyer
refused, claiming their Christian beliefs and constitutional
rights were being compromised in the detention home. "Boy,
Ron has him indoctrinated already," I said to Sally, "after just
a few weeks. Those sentences are straight out of Ron's

mouth." Finally, on Friday, the district judge ordered Ron and Janet to produce the girls or go to jail. Ron's lawyer turned the girls back over to state custody, barely five minutes before the judge's deadline ran out.

However, we knew that, in terms of trying to break the mind control Ron had over his daughters, we had lost more than a few days' progress. Allowing them back into Ron's clutches, even for a couple of days, was enough time for him to firmly reassert control over them. We who had lived in terror of him for so long and were still afraid of him after more than a year away from his grasp knew that all too well.

The other children were back in the hands of the state, but they were still too much under Ron's spell, and too frightened of him, to admit to any mistreatment at his hands. Also, we knew how difficult it would be for them to come out and say things against their own parents. That is a terrible thing for a child to have to do. It creates overwhelming guilt and anxiety, not to mention fear. But we also knew that somehow, we had to get them to break and come out with some details, some truth. After the first week, while the state was still struggling getting the girls back, Randall asked to be permitted to talk to his two youngest brothers, Luke and Mark. "I want to talk to them brother to brother, because then they might talk to the authorities, too. It's a long shot, but our only chance of getting them away from Ron permanently. It just might be what will help them open up and be truthful." Time was working against us. Given a longer period of time away from their parents and some heavy psychological counseling, the children would probably eventually break out of their prison of terror and tell the truth, as mine were doing, but we also knew we didn't have that kind of time.

Fortunately, the escape of the girls and Ron's refusal to return them made the judge more willing to listen to us. The court allowed us to visit Luke and Mark. Randall went alone on the first visit. After about an hour, Luke tentatively began opening up to him, telling him some things that had gone on since Randall left. The next day, Randall asked me to go with him, since the children had felt close to me. I went. The boys at first didn't recognize me. "Is it really you, Mary?" Mark asked me shyly. He was twisting his hands nervously together. "You look different. You don't look like yourself."

"I am different, Mark," I answered. "And I do look like myself. This is what I really look like when I'm away from that house. I hope you will be away from there, too, some day, and be happy like I am."

After that, I didn't press them or question them. I just let them lead the conversation in whatever direction they wanted, as the psychologist had advised me to do, and left any questions up to Randall. As we talked of inconsequential things, Luke, and then Mark, became more open and started to talk more easily about things that had happened to him, about how their father had beaten them and how frightened they were up in the attic when he made them all hide from the police. "Well, you need to tell the judge about all that," I said gently. "You know it's the truth about what happened, and you should never be afraid to tell the truth. God always wants you to be truthful."

Mark looked a little apprehensive. "You are safe now. Your father won't be allowed to hurt you anymore. You should tell the judge just what you've told us here," I said. Then I repeated, "It's the truth, you know that, and the judge will understand and know what to do. Don't worry. God won't hurt you, and He won't punish you, if you just tell the truth." I signaled to Randall that it was time for us to leave them now.

We hurried out to report to the court what had happened, and the judge agreed he would interview the boys himself. I was told I could testify to what I had heard the boys say in those sessions, and as a witness to what I had heard them admit to Randall. That day, they also took videotape testimony from Ellen, to be shown to the judge later. The judge, after talking to the boys himself, arranged for a psychologist to interview them. We all prayed for a break.

The prosecution called my son Jimmy to the stand. Jimmy's testimony electrified the court. He was so serious, so clean-cut sitting solemnly on the witness stand and cataloguing for them, in gripping detail, the torture he had suffered, or witnessed others suffer, living with Ron Larrinaga. Even the judge was obviously stunned.

The courtroom was hushed as my son Jimmy went on. "He'd come into the room with a Bible in one hand and a glass of whiskey in the other," said Jimmy, "and he'd calmly put the book down and then beat my mom until she couldn't stand up any more. One day, he made us all urinate in the toilet, and then he shoved my mom's head down in the toilet, into the urine." Jimmy told them about the constant beatings he had suffered, and the blood-spattered walls. He told them the terrible, terrible truth about our lives.

I was called to the stand after Jimmy and told them my own horrific experiences at Ron's hands. How he had my own sons and others like Kathleen beat me senseless. How I stood hour upon hour facing a wall, how he starved us, how he had mistreated all the children, and how he told me that he had simply abandoned June as "a child of the devil." My head bowed, tears falling, I admitted to the sexual acts he made me perform, and how powerful and terrible was the grip of mind control.

Louise, too, calmly testified to beatings, isolation, and sexual abuse, and how Ron had controlled her mind, and our minds, and how he still controlled the minds of those who lived with him day in and day out. She told the court how she had been able to regain her sanity and realize what Ron was only after years away from his influence, after he had ordered her shunned and called her a whore, and she cut off all contact with her family.

In the courtroom, Ron, meek and quiet looking in his suit and tie, with his steel-rimmed glasses and neatly parted and combed hair, sat and quietly read his Bible, seeming to pay no attention to the testimony of terrible abuse and molestation going on in front of him. He certainly didn't look capable of inflicting such cruel abuse on people, or of powerful mind control. Janet sat beside him, taking notes. I'll bet she hears it from him every night, I thought, remembering how brutally I'd be beaten if he thought I missed something in taking a note or writing a letter.

"As custody hearings go," said a television newscaster in a marvel of understatement, "this one is anything but routine."

Through it all, as testimony seesawed back and forth, and charges and counter charges of truth and lies were made, Sally kept cautioning us to restrain our optimism about Ron being removed permanently from his children's lives. "Remember, this is only a custody hearing on whether or not Ron will be allowed to keep his five youngest children. It is not a criminal trial, for no criminal charges have as yet been filed against him. And the older children are legal adults. No one will take them away from him."

That was a sobering comment. We were so glad to be finally telling our story to someone in authority, finally bringing out the truth, we had overlooked that fact. Ron Larrinaga would be free to go when the custody hearing ended. Whether or not he could take his younger children with him was the only issue before the court. All the other kids would still be under his domination no matter what happened here. I was outraged. "How can that be?" I wanted to know. "How can they possibly let a man like that go free, after what they've heard from all of us?" Our justice system didn't seem very "just" to me at that point.

Then it was Ron's turn, and, as we knew it would be, his defense had been carefully planned. Philip and Kathleen came to the witness stand one after the other to testify in Ron's behalf, vehemently denying that any abuse had ever occurred in their home, and claiming we were all lying. Philip was their star witness. He was so clean cut, so good looking, so *believable*.

"There was no abuse," he said, with great conviction. "We have a different lifestyle, but we live our lives according to the word of God." Under questioning, he admitted only that the children were "spanked once in a while with the back of a hairbrush." He denied there were any beatings, or other abuse and punishment. "The stories my mother and brother and sister told are all lies," he stated categorically. My heart sank when I heard that. But then, when the judge questioned Philip about his social life, and his friends, and whom he dated, Philip was stumped. He couldn't describe any normal social life a young man might enjoy, because he'd never had a date, he admitted, never gone out with a girl, never had a friend from a family other than ours. "I really don't know a lot of people my age," he finally stammered, lamely.

"Name even one," said the judge. Philip couldn't.

The court and the news reporters were also surprised to learn the real ages of Ron's older girls. They looked like young teenagers but were in their mid to late twenties, and dressed like twelve-year-olds. They weren't allowed to wear stockings, just turned down socks and loafers or patent leather shoes. They all wore their hair long, braided, flowing free, or tied back with big bows, or in curls with ribbons. They wore old-fashioned, long skirted cotton dresses, or skirts and blouses. To the modern eye, they looked very strange indeed.

"We live in a strict, protective, but violence-free environment," they testified. We knew those words had been hammered into them by Ron and looked at the judge hoping he too knew. The judge began questioning the girls specifically about their daily life, avoiding any references to beatings or sexual abuse, just asking normal questions about school and dates and such. As he did, the bizarre life they led became quite evident. The girls admitted they had never had a friend or a date, didn't know how to make a phone call, had never spent a night away from home, never gone to school, and did not have any friends outside their "family." One said, "I love my parents and would lay down my life for them." And though they all parroted Ron, claiming to be "good Christians, Baptists," none of them could identify what that was, or what Good Friday and Easter represented.

The second week of the trial was ending, and by then the media was abuzz over the incredible tale unfolding in the courtroom. Television and newspaper reporters from all over dogged our every step, and Ron took every possible opportunity to wave his red leather Bible at them and tell them, "I am the chosen servant of Jesus Christ, and these people are persecuting good Christian families. My children are held in captivity against their will. They are being made to do things they shouldn't do. Christ suffered from lies, and now I must suffer from these lies. 'Ye shall know the truth, and the truth shall make ye free.'"

But unknown to Ron, two younger boys had finally opened up to Judge Rickoff, telling him the truth. Their stories corroborated most of the testimony we had given, although they had not been in the courtroom to hear us. "The two boys have basically confirmed everything that everyone who has gotten out of that house has said, and have added some testimony about other experiences." The younger boys had told the judge that "life was horrible every day for them at home, and they never, ever, wanted to go back."

Then, after the judge ordered counseling sessions for them, too, three younger girls began telling their story, which confirmed what we had testified to in court. They also admitted to the fondling and sexual abuse they had endured at Ron's hands. Back in our hotel room, we cheered and pounded each other on the back. The case, we knew, was finally beginning to break.

Ron, though these latest developments must have shaken him, was still waving his Bible and denying everything, still assuring the eye of the television cameras it was all "religious persecution of the chosen servant of Jesus

Christ. God will prevail," he added significantly. I prayed earnestly for that to be true, that God *would* prevail, and see to it that this monster from hell impersonating His servant would receive the justice he deserved.

On December 1, our prayers were answered. Florida issued a warrant for Ron Larrinaga's arrest, on criminal charges of aggravated child abuse, aggravated sexual abuse, lewd and lascivious assault on a child, and several counts of physical and sexual abuse of me. A Texas marshal appeared at the end of testimony that afternoon and took Ron to a Texas jail, pending extradition to Florida. We learned later that his bond had been set at $50,000. We all breathed a little easier. We doubted he could raise that kind of money and that meant he couldn't run away.

Moreover, Florida had formally asked Texas to extradite him. His attorney commented to the reporters, "I don't think he'll be extradited. I don't think they have an adequate case on which to proceed with extradition."

Our hopes, so high, slipped a bit when we heard that, but Sally tried to buoy them. However, we didn't have much time to mull over that disappointment when a larger one overtook it. To our dismay, Ron managed to post bail almost immediately and was out on bond, able to maintain control over his remaining family members. But all was not well there, either.

On December 7, a bomb shell exploded, causing further newspaper headlines. Janet and her youngest daughter still out of custody asked to be taken into protective custody by the court. Already some of Janet's younger girls, after undergoing psychological counseling, had begun corroborating some of the stories about their father. We wondered, is

Janet really going to break, or is this a ploy of some sort that Ron has thought up? We didn't trust him for a second. However, as soon as Ruth was in protective custody, the judge ordered psychological counseling for her, too. The very next day, she began telling of beatings, abuse, and sexual molestation that had occurred. My heart went out to her, for I knew how terrified she must be, how fearful of retribution at her father's hands for this unforgivable transgression. Sure enough, when she got into court the next day and saw her father, she broke down, recanted her testimony, and mouthed, "I love you" to him.

But the judge already understood the truth. "I've heard enough," the judge said, overwhelmed and sickened. "No one in his right mind would turn children over to this man." But he agreed to let the case continue to be heard, so that his decision would not be overturned on appeal later.

That night, in front of the ever-present mob of television cameras and reporters, Ron, though nattily attired in a tan jacket and striped tie, seemed visibly shaken by this latest turn of events. However, he managed to mouth his usual diatribe. "My daughters have been forced to agree to these things," he declared. "The authorities are making them do things they shouldn't do, and say things they shouldn't say." We who were familiar with Ron recognized the note of hidden menace in his tone. "It's a setup. All my children are being influenced by evil people's lies!" I shuddered, knowing he would, without a doubt, brutally beat Ruth and the other children for this if he ever got them back in his clutches again!

I could only pray he wouldn't.

Then we heard reports that, based on the testimony

given by the children, Texas was considering filing criminal charges against Ron. We rejoiced.

"Do you have anything to say to that?" reporters asked Ron as he arrived for the day's testimony.

"I am suffering as Christ suffered when He was crucified, but it is a beautiful day," he replied. "They brought lewd and lascivious people, baser sorts, to bear witness against Christ, and so they have done now with me."

Finally, after nearly three weeks, the judge rendered his decision:

The five youngest Larrinaga children would remain in state custody for at least six months, until further investigations were made. "I am convinced these children suffered constant mental, physical, and sexual abuse," he said. "The unnatural isolation of the children is as great a factor in this as is the actual physical and sexual abuse." Ron Larrinaga was specifically barred by the judge from visiting his children. There would be a reevaluation in one month, said the judge, and, in the interim, the entire family was to undergo psychological evaluation.

We, and the Larrinagas' neighbors, were jubilant. "Fear has kept us prisoners in our own homes ever since they moved in," said one of the neighbors. "If they were outside, we stayed in. You know, they even painted lines in the street around their home, which we weren't supposed to cross. Weird! Now maybe our lives can get back to normal, and so can theirs, whatever normal is to people like that."

The Texas prosecutor made a rare public statement: "The amount of control and influence over these children was severe. Years of mind control are hard to erase. It takes a long, long time for victims in these situations to even admit to themselves what happened to them. We can help the younger children recover, but, for the older children, there are no agencies to offer them free help, even though it is obvious they desperately need it."

I could only agree with him, for it had taken me and my children over a year to begin to come to terms with ourselves, and start to face the horror of what had happened to us. The verdict helped. It vindicated our struggle to deal with the truth instead of the lies we had ingested for years. It had been a great victory for us, and hopefully it opened an escape hatch for the younger children of Janet and Ron Larrinaga, but none of us would feel safe until Ron was locked up where he could do no more harm to any of us.

12

further issues,
lingering spells

When we heard that Ron would be extradited to Florida to stand trial there on the criminal charges I had filed against him, we cried for joy. I hugged Sally Anderson. "I'm so grateful you listened to me that day."

"I'm glad, too," she said, "for the children especially. They've all suffered enough. Now we have to present a good case against him. But I also hear that Texas will be waiting in the wings when we get through with him. The district attorney is filing similar charges against Mr. Larrinaga here in Texas."

Overwhelmed with emotion, I had to sit down to absorb the impact of all that had happened in three short weeks. Tomorrow we'd be flying back to Florida, and Louise would head back to Germany. We had called Marian to tell her of the judge's decision, and she was thrilled. "I'll be there for the trial in Florida, Mom," she said. Randall and David would go back to California, where Randall intended to continue his search for his sister June, abandoned in Arizona all those years before. My son Jimmy decided to spend some time in Texas with friends, after a trip to California with Randall and David to see his father and Marian. Ellen and I would go back to Florida without him, and Ellen, to my great distress, would have to go back to Great Oaks Village to live when we got home.

The custody problem was still with me, but I felt sure that now that the story had surfaced in its ugly entirety, it would be easier to convince the judge to let me have my daughter back. I was wrong on that.

It took longer than I'd hoped, though we had both undergone a long period of psychological evaluation, and our psychologists unanimously recommended that Ellen be returned to my care. Ellen, who wanted to come home and live with me, had said so again and again. But finally Ellen was released from Great Oaks Village. What a day of celebration that was! She was to be closely monitored by the court, the judge ordered, and I was to continue counseling, and she was not to leave the state except with permission of HRS, and there were a lot of other restrictions, but I didn't care. I had my daughter again, and hopefully, with God's grace, a chance to establish some kind of normal life for her, something she had never known.

As fate would have it, on the same day I regained my daughter, the order of extradition of Ron Larrinaga, who had been kept in detention in the Texas jail after the custody trial, was granted, and he began his long, fateful journey back east for the trial. I read in the newspaper he was bound in chains for the trip.

Although I know that Christ did not teach us to rejoice at another's suffering, and I don't consider myself a vengeful person, I couldn't help being glad he suffered, just for a few days, some of what he made the rest of us suffer all those years. Anxiety! What did he know about terror and anxiety, or being in chains? He considered his extraditers "brutal and barbaric," but didn't consider what he had done to all of us wrong in any way. I just wanted to see him punished, the way we had been punished by him all those years. I wanted him to suffer the way we had suffered. I wanted him to hurt, to feel pain, the way we had all felt pain.

Shortly after he reached the Florida jail, Ron was moved to solitary confinement, where he remained for several weeks. Meanwhile, four of Ron's oldest children, still on his side, intended to testify for him at his trial. They moved to Florida to be near their father.

In Texas, Judge Rickoff assigned Janet a public defender and ordered her to undergo psychiatric examination and treatment. Afterward, she filed for a restraining order against Ron. Very soon after that, she filed for divorce. My sympathies were with her. She had suffered so much at her husband's hands.

In late February, a Florida judge assigned Ron a public defender, and the wheels that would carry him to trial slowly, ever so slowly, began to turn. The first hearing was set for the end of March, but as these things go, we were to learn, the name of the game is "delay, delay, delay." In our justice system, a large helping of patience and an ability to deal with waist-high stacks of paperwork, are prerequisites. After a while, I considered it a miracle that anyone ever lived long enough to see a case in our courts proceed from beginning to end. Things that should have taken only hours, or at most days, took months and years. The cost in time, human energy, and tax dollars was staggering.

Even though I knew there would be a lot to do to get ready for the trial, I also knew I had to keep my life on some kind of track, some even keel, for my sake and Ellen's. The first thing I did after I got custody of Ellen again was call my friend Olivia and share the happy news. "I'm so happy, Olivia, you can't imagine! And guess what? I've decided to move back to your area."

"Oh, Mary," she cried. "Do you mean it? I hope so!"

"Yes, I mean it. I'm going to look for a job there and a place to live for me and Ellen. Our own home!"

A few weeks later, I bought a used mobile home in a quiet residential park. Ellen and I moved in. Now that I had my esthetician's license, I was able to find a job with a local beauty salon. I didn't make very much, but Jack was paying me alimony and a small amount in child support every month, so that gave me at least some financial base.

Jack had been fair to me in our divorce settlement. When he sold the motor home, he sent me my share of the proceeds. I had put that into savings, and now I used some of it for a down payment on the mobile home and some to buy the electronic facial equipment I needed for work. We talked briefly after the Texas trial. Jack was glad I had gotten Ellen back, and that Ron had been arrested and our lives could go on in some normal way, but he was upset about Philip.

Jack agreed to make the payments on a newer car for me, and bought me a refrigerator for the mobile home, which was already furnished. I would get a share of the equity in the house in Tartola, if and when he ever sold it.

As I settled into my little mobile home, I prayed to God that this would be the last time I'd have to move. I just

232

wanted to settle down and provide a good home life for Ellen. But the next day, it was back to the ashes and the wicked stepfather. Ron, we learned from Philip and Kathleen, was creating as much uproar in jail as he had created in his own home. Whenever they put him in with other prisoners, he harangued and preached to them and carried on about being the chosen servant of Jesus Christ until they complained about it. The jailers were forced to move him elsewhere, or into protective custody or solitary. He bitterly complained to Philip, "What right does this jailer have to state to me that I am forcing my religion on these men?" We knew what that meant. "They accuse me because I attended the Bible study and put pressure on the teacher." We knew what that meant, too. Ron had taken issue with the teacher's "compromise with doctrine" like he always did. Now that he was in jail, away from us, the "lies and conspiracy" accusations were shifted to his jailers, and others in the prison system.

In May, after what seemed to me forever, the first pretrial hearing was held. It was a bond hearing, wherein Ron requested his bond be reduced from the $53,500 the judge had set. Jimmy flew in from Texas to testify again, and everyone lined up once more on their respective sides. We were surprised when Judge Rickoff flew in from Texas to testify against Ron being allowed out on bail. "I determined that your father was a very dangerous sociopath and a very dangerous person," he said.

Chuck Denton, the public defender for Ron, asked to be allowed to withdraw from the case, claiming that Ron accused him of not properly representing him. Also, he claimed, Ron refused psychological examination, which the

defender had asked he undergo to prepare a possible insanity
defense.

When the judge refused Mr. Denton's request to
withdraw, Denton began to attack me. He demanded to see
psychological reports on me. The prosecutors said no, not
without a court order. The judge refused to make that order.
Then Denton claimed that I was the "nutty one" and not
his client Ron.

"I think their victim in this case is crazy," he said. "If
there is a psychological report anywhere saying she is nutty,
I want to see it." I cried bitterly over that. Judge Antoon said
he wanted to see the transcripts from the Texas custody hearing, and ordered that Ron undergo psychiatric evaluation.
The DA won out, and Ron was bound over for trial without
reduction in bail. We breathed another collective sigh of
relief. The longer he was kept in jail, the better chance we
had of breaking through to the victims who still remained
firmly in Ron's thrall.

On June 14, Sally Anderson amended the criminal
charges against Ron. In addition to the six original charges
filed in November the previous year which involved me,
Jimmy, and Ellen, the state of Florida now filed forty-three
additional counts of aggravated child abuse, sexual battery,
lewd and lascivious assault upon a child, and child abuse.
This time, Ron's five minor children and my two minor children were brought into the suit.

Ron was formally accused, in the amended complaint,
of forcing the children to stand in closets or corners for more
than ten hours at a time, and sometimes for days at a time, of
manual sexual abuse on some of the girls using his fingers,
of illicitly fondling them, of beating them or ordering others

to beat them with belts or leather straps, and of inflicting physical and mental injury on the children.

It was during that hearing in May that we learned that Randall had finally succeeded in his search and had located his long lost sister June. A member of the Child Welfare Department in Arizona came to Florida to testify about Ron's abandonment of his daughter back years before, when school authorities stepped in. They reported that Ron had fled Arizona to avoid arrest by authorities and had simply left his daughter behind and never gave her a thought afterward.

June had spent the rest of her childhood as a ward of the state, being moved from foster home to foster home, and, from what Randall told us, she had never understood what happened or why she had been completely abandoned by her family. Randall went to see her, and she agreed to be a witness in Florida for the trial. I was anxious to see her again, but dreaded it. What would I say to her? How could I face her? Once more, though I had no control over what had happened to her, guilt overwhelmed me.

Time marched on, and so did the legal maneuvering. The defense filed for dismissal. They accused the prosecutors of threatening Kathleen Miller to make her testify. Meanwhile, I had to keep on with my daily life and somehow work and try to earn a living.

Ellen seemed to be doing well, now that she was out of the Village. She had become a normal child, good in her school work and enjoying her friends and our home. Though I wasn't making much money, my life was busy and full. I had begun to see a friend of Olivia's. Jim came and took me out to dinner on occasion, and I really looked forward to seeing him. Our relationship was beginning to blossom.

Most of all, I wanted the trial and my ties to Ron Larrinaga to be over with at long last. Deep down, though I tried not to admit it to myself, I still feared Ron with an unexplainable fear and dread. I feared that what I was experiencing now was just a dream, that he would someday, somehow come back and take control of my life again, and all this effort would go up in smoke. It had happened so often to me over the years, and no one could convince me it couldn't happen again.

The months flew by, and soon it was Christmas. My son David had come to Jim's house in Stuart from Fort Lauderdale, where he was working, to meet Jim. Ellen and I were at Jim's for Christmas Day. I was shocked and pleasantly surprised when Philip called me at Jim's and said he and Kathleen wanted to meet me that day and talk. They had completely avoided me since moving to Florida. We arranged to meet at Benjy's, a restaurant off the freeway in Fort Pierce, halfway between Stuart and Melbourne. I told them David was visiting, and Philip asked me to bring him along with me, so they could see him again.

That holiday lunch was the first acknowledgment of Christmas Philip had known since he was a little boy. Ron never permitted us celebration of Christmas, or celebration of any kind, for that matter. And even though it was in a fast-food restaurant off a major freeway and Philip was still pretty well on Ron's side, not mine, it was very special. Philip seemed glad to see his brother David again. We tried not to dwell on the trial, but before he and Kathleen left, I said to them earnestly, "You both have to try to come out from under Ron's spell. I'm telling you the truth about what happened, and about what he has done, and so are Ellen and Jimmy and the others. Deep inside, you *know* it's the truth, and you *know* what really happened to you, but he still has you totally under his control, and he will for as long as you continue to visit him. You must listen to me. You have to stop seeing him. That's the only way you'll ever break his hold on you. And you just have to let yourselves come to the truth within you about what he has done, as the Lord wants you to do. God will help you in this, if you will let Him and trust yourselves to Him, away from Ron."

Philip later said it was only a couple of weeks after that Edward Larrinaga called him. "Philip," Edward said, "I've been talking to Ruth and Kathleen."

"Yeah? What about?"

"Well, you know the stuff about my dad having sex with your mom and all the girls, molesting them and that stuff?"

"Yeah. What about it?"

"Well, Kathleen says it's all true. She says that Dad had sex with your mom and did things to her and to Ruth, too. Kathleen swears it's the truth."

After that, bit by bit, Philip allowed the true situation to come into the light of his heart and mind. Once he was reasonably able to face it, he was able to go with Kathleen and Edward to the state's attorney and cooperate with the authorities in the case. Sally Anderson had been transferred to another area of Florida, so they called on Gayle Mullens and told her what had happened to them. She said, "Well, you came out of the mist just in time. We're hoping for a May court date on this."

Then Philip called me, and I cried when he told me he was ready to testify for me and his sisters. "Oh, Philip, I'm so happy, and Louise and Marian will be happy, too, when they hear this. I'm so glad you are finally facing the truth, and I love you and feel so responsible! I'm just glad you're finally out from under his control for good and can live your life. It will get better, Philip, you'll see. God will help you handle it."

Despite my reassurances, it wasn't easy. Philip still had doubts and misgivings, as did Edward and Kathleen, but as time went on their convictions about Ron's culpability became stronger and so did they. "It's just ourselves and our own lives we're unsure of now," Philip said. "Our entire value system has just been kicked out from under us, and there is no safety net to fall into."

No one had more sympathy for them than I did. For their agony even now was mine. I tried to reach out to them as best I could. Meanwhile, Randall had been busy out in California. He contacted his bother Bobby, whom we hadn't seen since he'd run away from the beatings Ron inflicted on him, and lined him up to testify against Ron at the trial. Jack still didn't want to be involved again, and we agreed we didn't really need him. The DA could always subpoena him if we did. My Louise and Marian were both ready to testify. Waiting for the trial to begin was difficult for all of us. It seemed like a mirage, something that would never become reality. Delay after delay, motion after motion, confirmed our uncertain feelings.

Now over a year had passed since the Texas hearing, over a year since Ron had been extradited to Florida. The waiting became more unbearable. Yet, I rationalized, in another way it was a godsend. In that interval, the children gained time to begin to come out from under Ron's control and think for themselves again. And the period of delay gave Philip, Kathleen, Ruth, and Edward time to recant their earlier testimony, to see the truth. God, I guessed, knew what He was doing. Finally, in early April, I received a call from the state's attorney. "Ron's criminal trial is on the docket and will begin soon, probably May."

We began getting ready, gathering witnesses, who by then were scattered all over the United States. The state's attorney, handling the prosecution, hoped to convict Ron based on the evidence of his abuse of his own children and the mind control he had exerted over them. Having Kathleen especially, and Philip and Edward, who had testified for him before, ready to recant and testify against him, was a big plus for the prosecution, even though they knew the defense would make a major counterattack about that and try to destroy their credibility as witnesses.

Because of Chuck Denton's attack on me, they hoped not to have to call me, Ms. Mullens said. Ron's own children would be the front line of attack. They decided to charge Ron with forty-three counts of child abuse.

Gayle Mullens told me they'd probably call Jimmy, since his testimony had been so effective in Texas, but would try to spare Ellen from taking the stand, if they could. "I'm grateful for that," I said. "This is so hard on her."

"Then, if all here fails," Ms. Mullens said, "which I don't think it will, he has Texas to face again, don't forget." She raised my spirits and made me feel confident again.

However, they were dashed when what we all feared most surfaced. Ron's attorney wanted to plea bargain with the prosecution. His client would plead "no contest" to a number of the counts of aggravated child abuse, sexual battery, and lewd and lascivious assault on a child, he said, in exchange for an eight-year sentence, and twenty-two years of probation. The prosecutors tentatively agreed, but the final decision would be up to the judge assigned to the case, Judge Cross.

My morale plunged and my heart dropped when we learned that, under Florida's early release laws and given the year he had already spent in prison, if the judge accepted the plea bargain, Ron Larrinaga would be out of jail in eight months or less! He'd be free by Christmas!

When she heard that, Gayle Mullens asked to withdraw from the plea agreement. "Our intention was that this man actually serve the eight years," she told the judge. "When we found out that would not happen, we decided to withdraw the plea." To our relief, the judge refused to accept the plea bargain. They offered Ron a new one: twenty-five years in prison, twenty-five years on probation. That would mean he'd serve at least eight or nine years of prison, allowing the youngest Larrinaga children to reach majority before he was released.

My spirits plunged again. They had no idea! With a man like Ron, eight years was nothing! He'd be back working on me and those kids the day he got out and wouldn't rest or leave us alone until he had us all under his domination again and had taken his revenge on us. But this time, Ron himself refused to accept the new plea bargain offer.

Then the defense attorneys questioned Ron's mental competence to stand trial and act in his own defense, and the judge ordered competency hearings. Ron kept trying to interrupt the judge all during the hearings and complained endlessly about his attorneys, demanding to be allowed to talk to the media about them, and loudly asserting he was going to complain to the Florida Bar Association. We knew it was just part of his usual "uproar" tactics, but we worried that they might think he was incompetent and he would escape punishment again. Once again, the waiting was intolerable. Finally, on May 10, Ron was determined to be competent enough to stand trial. The defense asked for another delay. Our hearts sank and then rallied when the judge denied it. At last, a firm trial date was set, beginning the following week. Ms. Mullens told us she expected the trial to last several weeks, maybe a month. She had more than thirty witnesses to call.

Despite the occasion, I joyfully welcomed my reunion with Louise and Marian when they arrived for the trial. They were pleased that Ellen was finally at home with me and we all savored the time together, even though it was engendered by such painful circumstances. Jimmy came from Texas, and the others from California. David came up from Fort Lauderdale. Jack did not come. He had a new life, a new wife, and a new family. Jim gave me his full moral support and said he would come up and attend some of the court sessions, since as a possible witness I was barred from going into the courtroom during the trial.

Last minute legal maneuvering and jury selection took days. But finally, on May 18, Ron Larrinaga's criminal trial began. Anxiously, we prepared ourselves for the ordeal ahead. Would justice finally prevail?

13

the jury speaks

Before a hushed Florida courtroom, Dana Larrinaga told of a life filled with constant beatings, isolation, and sexual molestation by Ron. "He would preach, and he would yell, and he would hit. He'd ask us questions, and, if we couldn't answer, we'd be beaten severely." She described how Ron had come home one day with a magazine that had an article in it about a girl who had taken drugs and later was beaten to death. Her father insisted the article was a message from God, telling him he should beat his children. "He told my older sister, 'Beat them for every little thing they do. Beat them until they can't stand.'"

She told of the welts, the bruises, the swelling that lasted for days after these beatings. She told how her father came into the bathroom when she was in the shower, fondled her, and played with her sexually, claiming he was doing it for Jesus Christ, and had done those things to her since she was a little girl not more than seven years old. She told how she had seen him do similar things to others, to her brothers and sisters, to me, and to my children. She told of never having gone to school. Her testimony was confirmed and repeated again and again, by different children, with different examples, but all with the same theme of unrelenting torment, isolation, brainwashing, and abuse at the hands of their father.

Every day I got up in the morning, dressed and fixed myself up carefully, and made the long drive north to the county courthouse where the trial was taking place, in case I was called as a witness. None of us were permitted to talk to each other: the judge had imposed a strict gag order. We were extra careful because we didn't want anything to go wrong. Finally, after what seemed like an eternity, both sides had finished presenting their cases, and closing arguments began.

The close, humid air, normal in June, seemed even more intense that Friday as I guided my car into a vacant spot in the courthouse parking lot. My motions were almost mechanical. Although I had been doing the same thing every morning for weeks while the trial dragged on, today there seemed to be a different current in the air, an electricity that was almost palpable. As I locked my car, I stared up at the aging white courthouse baking placidly in the sun. It stood there in silence, impervious to the heat, and to the trial and traumas inside. If only it could talk, I thought, what stories it could tell about the lives hanging in the balance within its walls.

I was determined but tense, anxious at facing Ron, feeling the same clenching and burning in my stomach that had been there daily since the trial started. Inside, in the semi-cool of the overworked air conditioner struggling against the constant opening of the door, I began my familiar routine pacing, up, down, up, down the long hallway.

Brilliant sunlight streamed in from a window high above me, reflecting harshly off the hard terrazzo floor. Tic-tac, tic-tac, my high-heeled patent leather shoes echoed in the silence. Reaching the wide, closed doors of the courtroom, I stopped before them and stared, agonizing, wanting it all to end. Not a sound emerged from behind those doors. Not a person appeared. It was eerie. I felt helpless and alone, and very, very frightened.

Suddenly, bile rose in my throat, and I felt a choking sensation. Fear engulfed me. I needed air. Tic-tac, tic-tac, tic-tac, I hurried toward the door. Stepping outside, the heat struck me like a fist, and I flinched. I felt a wave of nausea and shivered as bumps rose along my arms. Leaning into the tiny sliver of shade offered by one of the fat pillars at the top of the steps, I touched my head to its chipped stone surface, seeking the relief of a coolness that wasn't there. Then I moved away and anxiously smoothed my rumpled clothes. I had dressed carefully that morning in the new raspberry linen skirt I had made the week before and a matching floral blouse. I wanted to look my best today—crisp and clean and confident—since the case was to go to the jury. But I probably looked as gray, sweaty, and bedraggled as I felt.

Thankfully, the reporters were leaving us alone, not like in Texas where they had dogged our every step. With Judge Cross's gag order to protect the children in effect they knew it was useless to try to talk to any of us. I reached up and lifted away a strand of hair clinging damply to my neck, praying for a breeze to come and cool things, just a little.

I glanced around. Law offices circled the courthouse, like a wagon train positioned to fight off invaders. Though it was the county seat and highly touted as the "doorstep to space," Titusville, viewed from the steps of its courthouse, offered little to the eye that lived up to its lofty name. A plane glided by, a small shadow in the vast blue of the sky above. Like everything else about this day, and about this case, it moved in slow motion. To the west, from the direction of Orlando, fluffy white clouds piled up like giant snow banks, a sure sign there'd be a thunderstorm that afternoon.

By the time those clouds reached here, I knew, they'd be sooty and ominous, with streaks of lightning randomly shooting from their rain-swollen depths. They'd dump their burden on us, most likely, before hastening out across the nearby Atlantic. Florida's afternoon thunderstorms were renowned for their ferocity. But a good rain would be welcome, I thought, if only it would bring a bit of cool relief. Turning, I fled again into the relative comfort of the courthouse.

The case was finally with the jury. Standing again before the doors to the courtroom, I was tempted to pull them open and go in, but I didn't dare. I probably now could go in without penalty, but I wasn't really sure. Better not risk it, I decided.

I wished one of my children was with me. I needed company, someone to hang onto during this long tense vigil. I hadn't realized how hard it would be to wait it out alone. But those who had come to testify were either sequestered away in separate witness areas, or had testified and left.

I wandered back to the small windowed alcove off the main hallway. Half a dozen straight-backed chairs offered uncomfortable seating. They were all filled. There was no reading material there. As the minutes, then hours, ticked by, I wished for even a dull government pamphlet to read. I decided to go in search of a book, a magazine, anything to take my mind off what was happening in that courtroom.

Another hour crawled glacially past. I couldn't stand the tension of waiting. Restlessly, I resumed pacing the hall. Just then, the doors to the courtroom flew open. Reporters streamed out, dashing for the few telephones. I grabbed one young, red-haired man by the arm. "What happened?" I asked breathlessly. "What was the verdict?" Waiting for his answer, my heart seemed to stop. I could feel the blood pounding in my ears. I felt like I was going to faint.

"GUILTY!" he shouted excitedly. "On all forty-two counts! Guilty!" and raced off in search of a free telephone.

I stood there, stunned, trying to grasp the significance of what he had just said. The jury had found Ron Larrinaga guilty! Relief, sudden and powerful, sucked the air from me. I gasped and leaned against a wall for support. "Oh, thank you, Lord," I breathed. "Thank you!"

Tears poured down my cheeks, but I was oblivious to that. I just stood there crying as people rushed past me. I felt dizzy, ecstatic, disoriented. It was over, it was really over, at long last. I should go home, I thought. I'm free now, and safe. I need time to think about what this means, for them, for me, for all of us, especially the children.

Until this moment, I feared that justice would never have a chance. I had begun to doubt the whole system and was convinced that this monster who had warped and shattered our lives would never be tried for his crimes. My greatest fear was that Ron Larrinaga would not be convicted and would, somehow, be freed. That he'd get out and be free to try to harm us again, free to attempt to wreak havoc on our lives, and the children's lives.

I walked slowly to my car, got in, and turned the key in the ignition. Now, as I drove home, the rain finally came, like my tears, in washing torrents. It drummed down on the car roof, as lightning flashed and thunder crashed all around me. The windshield wipers clicked and whooshed as I squinted, trying to see through the slanting sheets of rain, hunching forward, hands clenched on the steering wheel. I turned the radio on and fiddled to find a newscast. Finally I found one. I strained to hear through the static the storm was creating.

The newscaster was reading off details about the Larrinaga case. "The listing of all the charges, each with its response of 'Guilty!' from the foreman of the jury, took more than a quarter of an hour. The defendant, who claims he is a preacher and a 'chosen servant of Jesus Christ,' calmly read his Bible throughout the verdicts, never once looking up at the jurors. Then, in a move that surprised the court, the foreman asked to read a message from the six member jury to the children, all victims of Larrinaga's abuse. The judge granted the request. The foreman then read this statement: 'We hope the children move on from their experiences of abuse and lead fruitful lives.'" The newscaster breathlessly emphasized that Larrinaga had been convicted on all forty-two counts. Silently, I thanked God for this victory.

As I pulled into the carport next to my mobile home, the rain stopped and the sun appeared, glistening on the wet grass. I could see cows and horses peacefully grazing in fields nearby. Everything looked washed and clean, exactly the way I felt now, washed and cleaned again. Our long ordeal was over. Ronald Larrinaga would never harm his children, or me, or anyone again. After years and years of unrelenting misery, we were finally safe.

epilogue

On Friday the thirteenth, a Bible-waving Ronald Joseph Larrinaga, self-proclaimed chosen servant of Jesus Christ, was sentenced to 180 years in prison on forty-two counts of sexual molestation and child abuse. His subsequent appeal was denied, and he is now serving his sentence in Florida's Marion Correctional Institute.

Fortunately, all of Larrinaga's victims, twenty of them children, lived. They escaped, or were eventually rescued, but not before great harm had been done to them. The children were totally innocent victims. They had no choice. They were trapped in a living hell on earth. And the long-range effects of this terror-filled environment are just becoming known.

I am trying to rebuild my life, to chase away Ron's ghost, to build a better future, and, though I am much better now, I still haven't turned that final corner. Many of the children have barely begun the journey. And for most, the beginning has been filled with emotional and physical pain. There are many ongoing hardships. For them it will be a long and treacherous road, with no past to hang onto and an unknown future to reach for.

Ron has not given up trying to control those who had been part of the cult and especially the children, even from behind bars. He has written long letters to Philip, Kathleen, and Edward, filled with religious invective and threats of what God's punishment on them will be for betraying him. They showed me some of the letters. "I was recognized by Mary and her husband as a Minister of the Gospel of Jesus Christ," he wrote to Philip. "Your father began to be alienated from Mary when their Christian beliefs conflicted. He did not sleep with his wife, but chose to dissipate himself at school with the girls, in stimulating himself . . ."

I have tried to reassure my children that these words are lies, that their father is a good man who has always loved them and who tried to be a good husband to me though I misguidedly led them all into Ron's evil web. And though we are no longer together, he has continued to fairly support me in our divorce settlement, showing his own compassion and generosity.

Jim and I continued seeing each other, on the weekends we could manage it, and I slowly progressed through beauty school, although I had some difficulty concentrating and doing the mathematical calculations required. I was diagnosed with "post-traumatic stress syndrome," and they told me that constant tiredness was one of the symptoms of that.

As the survivor of terror and personal tragedy, even though it was a tragedy partially of my own making, I am determined now to continue to move forward. I am going to make it, I will make it, and I pray daily that the others and especially my children and the Larrinaga children will find the emotional stability to rebuild their lives, too.

None of us can undo the past. We must look to the future. Each person must reach up for God's help to rescue them, and I pray daily that the others will find the strength and courage to do that. I also pray that everyone who finds themselves trapped in a similar situation will find that same strength.

The judge was right when he looked Ron Larrinaga in the eye and said, "You are not answering to the Almighty here, you'll report to Him later." Justice on earth has begun. It will end only when Ron Larrinaga finally comes face to face with his Maker.

Many times I think about my own gullibility about Ron Larrinaga's hold over us. How did it happen? I ask myself, for the millionth time. How could I have been so stupid, so naive? Was it my lack of self esteem, my desire for a prophet to lead us into religious perfection? How could I not have seen what this man was, what we were getting into? But no matter how often my mind screams it, there is never an acceptable answer. How indeed? It is a question that will haunt me for the rest of my days.

I realize that I cannot singlehandedly undo the damage, or mend the terrible injustice of our lives. The stress of my past and the uncertainty of my future continue to take their toll on my physical strength, but maintaining a positive attitude enables me to carry the load of everyday life, with God's help. I am grateful for that, and progressing. I have been able to let go a bit, let myself rise, and allow the children to grow as they must and find their own way in life.

Though I will always be there to support them.

As painful as it has for me to relive these events on these pages—to reexamine in detail my motivations and my soul, to re-experience the nightmare of those days—if it exposes the tactics of cult leaders like Ron Larrinaga, if it helps one family understand, or saves one child from the horror and hell in which we lived for so long, it will have been well worth it.

afterword

By Robert T. Cross, Ph.D., Psychotherapist

The terms "cult" and "cultist" are familiar words to us now, regularly bandied about in the media. But what exactly *is* a cult? And who, or what, is a cultist? Webster defines a cult as "a system of beliefs and rituals connected with the worship of a deity, a spirit, or a group of deities." That, by definition, encompasses *every* religion, or belief system, on earth. A cultist is a follower of, or believer in, such a religion or system. So it is difficult to specifically define what we in our society truly mean when we use the words "cult" or "cultists." Perhaps the extended definition more clearly identifies it: "A great or excessive devotion or dedication to someone, idea, or thing." Now we are closer to the meaning assigned by most of us to the words cult and cultist. Excessive (or extreme) are the key words. We assign the label "cult" to any system in which the worship, ritual, or behavior is what we consider "excessive," that is, outside the bounds of normal society, or that carries its beliefs to an extreme—again, to an extent beyond that which the average person might deem reasonable. Often such extremism has horrifying or tragic results. Thus it is that we, for the most part, associate the terms "cult," and "cultist," with abnormal, aberrant, or supernatural activities or behavior. Behavior outside the norm.

253

In the story of Mary Rich and Larrinaga, Ron Larrinaga exemplifies in microcosm the type of extremist cult leader who demands complete subjugation and submission from his followers. Larrinaga espoused, and then promulgated to others, his perceived direct relationship with, and orders from, the Almighty, and used that as rationale to superimpose his will and domination on his victims. In his mind, he answered not to this world, nor to the laws of society, but to a higher authority, and his superior knowledge of Biblical injunction. Those two powers accorded him, in his victims' minds, the absolute, unquestionable right to ignore society's laws and dole out whatever punishments he saw fit for their committed sins and transgressions against his, and God's, authority. They *believed* that his authority came directly from God, and that it was a sin for them to question it, or rebel against it. In this belief, Larrinaga controlled his followers under the guise of helping them on their journey to eternal peace—the ultimate reward or goal they sought. Any resulting or deliberate abuse of innocent children under his control was couched in what he perceived as his inalienable right to practice religion and train or punish children in the manner that he, and his followers, wished.

We can ask ourselves what psychologically propels—or impels—people who are average, supposedly normal human beings, into believing the ideas and accepting the manipulations and deceptions of an extremist leader? An over-simplified explanation would be that the follower gains a great measure of emotional gratification in belonging to a group that feels and thinks the same way he or she does. There is also the luxury of relinquishing personal responsibility—of allowing oneself to be dependent on another, or on others, to make difficult decisions about one's life and routine—to provide sustenance, both physical and spiritual, in one's day to day life—and it is also tempting to avoid culpability for one's actions, by simply "following orders." Belonging and sharing are powerful motivators. However, these notions do not explain the deeper motivation of the cult member which bonds together the cult's extreme beliefs and behaviors, and which ultimately forms a life-or-death type struggle.

Cult leaders may, in some instances, be psychiatrically disturbed, but their followers are not usually psychiatrically disturbed, in the sense that they do not fit into some neat diagnostic category. For the most part, cult followers are average people who have lived a fairly normal life before joining a cult (unless born into it), and who experienced the same degrees of depression and anxiety that most of us experience in coping with our lives. What sets them apart from the average person is the deep sense of hopelessness. Hope then becomes the catalyst between what they themselves seek, and the beliefs within the cult. What the cult leader does, through manipulation of the individual, is set in motion the hopeful belief that by joining a cult, the person will find the inner peace or goal that he or she unconsciously seeks. The cult leader represents that hope, and manipulates followers with that hope.

It is the lack of hope, intertwined with the individual's own belief system, that gradually opens the door for cults to attract and keep members. It is through the offer of hope, or a solution to what is perceived as discouragement, or pervasive disappointment with their lives, their world, or their future, that allows these extremists to prey upon and attract potential members, and then maneuver them into accepting radical or aberrant beliefs and actions. Obviously, the process of conversion takes time and intense attention. Through emotional appeal and personal charisma, the leaders convince their followers that only through the cult will they ever realize the inner peace or goal they seek. Only through the cult will they find hope again.

Another step is to gradually limit the individual's freedom, and to eventually isolate them from outside contact that might deter them from following the leader. Thus the individual's belief system becomes more and more closely aligned with the cult's. Once converted, the individual's beliefs, thoughts, and behavior are rigidly defined, controlled, inculcated and reinforced on a daily basis. Other beliefs and thoughts are carefully, systematically purged. Finally, total immersion in the cult's belief system is achieved.

This total immersion—total commitment to the social, emotional, sexual, political, and physical behavior code of the cult, and

the adoption of its radical belief system—is what makes it so difficult for members to ever leave. They are imprisoned in the system
not by physical walls or bars or barriers, but by the walls and fears
inculcated in their minds.

As we have seen in this account, escape and recovery from
cult attachment is an extremely difficult and harrowing process for
all involved, and sadly, once escape is accomplished, recovery is
not always achieved. The failure rate is very high. Once out of the
cult, by whatever method, victims are often unable to restabilize
their lives, and require extensive and ongoing therapy to cope with
the world outside the cult. For those whose adjustment prior
to entering the cult was marginal, the exiting could conceivably
precipitate a psychological breakdown, requiring psychiatric
hospitalization. The difficulty stems from leaving a structured
environment, where close relationships have been developed. The
ex-cultist feels alone, frightened, and rejected. What was a hopeful
belief is now challenged. They must relinquish what they wanted
most—the belief in achieving eternal peace. Cult values they so
intensely adopted are questioned, further destabilizing a fragile
value system. This in particular may account for why so many
ex-cultists experience a floating sensation. There are questions of
who to trust, from which may issue a sense of suspicion and distrust.
Most importantly, by leaving the cult they see the loss of what
little hope they had in finding the internal comfort, or the goal of
religious perfection. The new-found freedom also carries with it
the responsibility of caring for themselves, and making decisions
for and about themselves, which they are ill equipped to handle. It
is no easy task for any of us, but for someone that has been shel-
tered and rigidly supervised, and has become totally dependent, this
can be a monumental hurdle. The common emotional responses
for an ex-cultist are fear, anxiety, anger and/or depression. The
challenge for those assisting in the recovery is to provide a stable,
trusting, emotional support system for the ex-cultist.

Mary and most of her children, as well as Larrinaga's son,
experienced the majority of these problems when leaving the cult.
Fortunately, they have managed to make a fairly successful re-entry

to the world, once they were removed from the influence of Ron Larrinaga. That they have continued to progress is probably due to extended deprogramming and therapy, and because Larrinaga is safely shut away from them in prison, unable to now exert his influence over them, or instill fear in them on a daily basis. Not all victims in this story have managed to make as successful a recovery, but they are all doing the best they can.

Mary's story showed us the chaotic lives of people who, by falling under the spell of a demented cult leader, supply the means for themselves and their children to be assimilated and abused. They were tyrannized, abased, and physically tortured, yet their acceptance of that violent abuse was, for the most part, acquiescent and passive. In most cases of severe abuse and torture, the victim is not a willing participant. The abuse and torment are imposed against their will. Cultism defeats that logic. The victims are not only accepting, but seem to seek personal and physical degradation as a means of atonement for imagined sins. Most cult leaders use this religious dissatisfaction as the vehicle to gain their true objective: total control over their intended followers and victims. The adults are seeking not just religious security and "freedom," but, as in this case, realization of a fantasy of religious perfection. In Mary's case, that fantasy provided the means which Larrinaga, a twisted and dangerous sociopath, used in his quest for his victims. Often times, especially in the cultist atmosphere where mind control is total, the persecuted becomes the prosecutor, and that is what happened with the older children in this situation as well. The adults, and the older children, complied with Larrinaga's desires and demands to the utmost, and obeyed in the demanded torture and tyrannization of the younger children whenever they "misbehaved" or seemed to stray from the cult leader's rigid rules.

Why did Mary and the other cult victims do nothing to extricate themselves from these bizarre and abusive situations? One can only speculate that their victimized behavior is associated with a deeper and more elusive psychological motivation.

The leader's religious paranoia pushes him to extremes of behavior. The leader or the appointed enforcers dole out severe

punishment or retribution to recalcitrate followers or "unbeliev-
ers," believing that they have a God-given right to do so, up to and
including acts that result in fatalities.

Followers accept cruel and brutal punishment, for they
believe the leader or his appointed enforcers have that right, and
they submit themselves and their children to their will.

For Mary, membership in the cult took on such an intensity
and centrality in her life that it regulated all other motivations—
permeating relationships, influencing significant decisions, and
impairing her ability to act on sound judgment or to behave in such
a way that protected her children from harm.

This is merely a brief overview, a sketchy profile of an
extremely complex phenomenon in society today. Admittedly, it
raises more questions than it answers. However, in view of the
alarming rise in the number and variety of extremist cults in modern society, with more and more people turning themselves and
their lives, and more importantly the lives and welfare of their
hapless children, over to the control of zealots who may be determined sociopaths, we might do well to ask what impels so many to
a sense of hopelessness and despair, one so great that they seek
realization of fantasies in following cults? Also, we must ask how
we, as a rational society, should or might confront and address
those issues in a way that will prevent more abuses like the
tragedies of Mary Rich, her children, and the Larrinaga children, as
well as the tragedies of Guyana, Waco, Oklahoma City, Tokyo, and
others. If not, such horrifying abuse will continue and might even
become more frequent.